Unlocking the Mystery of You

The Pinnacle of Purpose

D. L. Anderson

authorHOUSE®

AuthorHouse™
1663 Liberty Drive
Bloomington, IN 47403
www.authorhouse.com
Phone: 1-800-839-8640

Published by AuthorHouse   10/22/2014

ISBN: 978-1-4969-3126-9 (sc)
ISBN: 978-1-4969-3125-2 (e)

Library of Congress Control Number: 2014948579

CONTENTS

DEDICATION

*

I dedicate this book to my dearly departed brother, by family and by faith,
Mark Lewis Anderson, who during the closing days of his life showed
me the undying power of purpose and the true meaning of destiny.

FOREWORD

*

Have you ever stopped to think? I mean have you *really* stopped to think; specifically about something or someone who meant a great deal to you, someone or something which really mattered? If so, how long was it until you were being pulled away into addressing another concern which for that moment seemed to be more important yet really wasn't?

Unfortunately this example is a common reoccurrence in many of our lives. In fact, I surmise nearly 80% of everything we do is unnaturally necessary. That is to say, most of our actions are indeed necessary, but not because nature has made them this way. Rather they have evolved into necessities in large part due to the social and economic tenors of our world, many of which contradict various laws of nature.

Let's talk about our world. At present, our world is tragically devolving into a collection of exclusive societies delineated by a sharp skew between those who "have" and those who "have not." Additionally, as the boundaries segregating these societies are as broad as the skew is sharp, only a minority of our world population has a clear path to fulfilling their purpose in life.

This undesirable variance is but one of several challenges associated with the legendary quest for fulfillment. Thus although this well-known pursuit is indeed life's most worthwhile endeavor, it is a proposition of epic proportion. This is not solely because of the complexities involved, but more so because of the immense value of fulfillment (which is why I tend to believe it is the greatest of life's few great rewards).

Noticeably fulfillment will be a common theme throughout this guidebook, a compilation of lectures I personally consider as a "seeker's guide to fulfillment." Strategically each chapter leads you further down the path which not only concludes with fulfillment; this particular path also provides each seeker with varying levels of fulfillment as they dedicatedly travel this select way.

This speaks to the relevancy of this work, for fulfillment is the successful conclusion of every authentic purpose and purpose is the chief component of relevant living. Therefore, to accomplish the task of helping each seeker find fulfillment, it is crucial to first and foremost delineate an applicable model of purpose (the model being equated to the aforementioned path). As such, all who do seriously contend for the prize of fulfillment will inevitably become seekers of purpose (i.e. purpose seekers).

Now the question each purpose seeker must ask individually (and one which I asked myself before compiling this work) is this – what makes this literature unique as it pertains to the countless books (most of them beyond credible and worthy) which have afore been written on purpose, fulfillment, and numerous related concepts?

Ultimately the answer lies in the thorough validation of a comprehensive model of fulfillment – and after years of study, I have formulated such a model which perfectly accounts for the unique relationship between fulfillment and purpose. Thus naturally, I have designated it as the *"Pinnacle of Purpose."*

Structurally the Pinnacle of Purpose takes on the form of a mountain, being illustrated by ascending levels representing our progressive evolution into our unique destiny (which in this context is equated to the "detailed version" of our purpose).

Definitively the Pinnacle of Purpose is founded upon a universal message represented by a collection of correlating principles which speak to some of the most imperative topics germane to the progressive existence of man and his intrinsic search for meaning.

Decisively the Pinnacle of Purpose is illustrated by a purposeful roadmap which guides each one following to a place where they can experience the fulfillment they seek – and as the divine texts would put it, that more abundantly.

The alternative in my opinion is unacceptable, and I wish I could go as far as to say unthinkable. Yet I am not ignorant on this wise, for I have come to know many who are living under continually difficult circumstances. Sadly these adverse circumstances not only increase the obscurity of their path to fulfillment. They also increase their need for purpose; particularly a reason to continue to press their way through constant hardship, and a cause to endure the daily toil of their spirits and the wearing of their souls.

I am also a student of history. Hence I am constantly reminded of the horrors of some of man's darkest days, whether by study or by simply observing the effects which many of these depraved deeds and indifferences have had on our present society.

Take the Holocaust, for example, and reason within yourselves the difficulty, villainy, and utter humility involved with such an inhumane experience. Or consider the Trans-Atlantic Slave Trade and the unimaginable living conditions of those forced into a life of slavery.

Believe me; the regrettable conclusion you will come to is as sad as it is sure. Unequivocally, history is filled with numerous accounts of some of the most unforgiveable moments and near unthinkable crimes – and each one bears a tragic lot of countless victims whose potential of experiencing fulfillment was contracted beyond measures deemed impossible. Indefensibly the decrease in their prospects of fulfillment (whether gradual or sudden) was so drastic that they ultimately became non-existent.

All things considered, it's difficult to determine how much farther along we truly are as a world populace as it pertains to the all-encompassing scale of fulfillment. On this wise, it's not enough to say we've moved beyond some of the inexcusable treacheries of yesteryear. No sir; as a progressive society we must also come to a place where everyone has a fair shot at finding fulfillment and ultimately fulfilling their purpose.

As for me, my purpose in life is not necessarily to affect legislation in the order of institutionalizing a level playing field for all who seek fulfillment. My purpose (at least one of them) is to simply reveal what I believe is the most comprehensive path; especially for those who are so exasperated with the status quo and the emptiness of their current station that they have, metaphorically speaking, packed their bags and are alone searching for a way out.

To these and all others who I am convinced will benefit from all the words recorded on the following pages, I have given my best effort to delineate a universal model of fulfillment – and I believe I have. Subsequently the model of the Pinnacle of Purpose is not merely in concept. It is in application and ready to be utilized by anyone who is ready to walk the path to fulfillment.

I can state this with certainty because I have employed and verified the effectiveness of the Pinnacle of Purpose in my own life. Thus I am not merely an author speaking to an abstract ideal I've conjured up into some semi-elaborate model. I am also a witness to its usefulness per my current levels of fulfillment and success.

Notwithstanding, my personal verification of this model is secondary to its universal nature. As a matter of fact, the universality of the Pinnacle of Purpose is not only the most crucial factor of this model; it is also the highest form of relevant evidence I could offer in support of this composition. Else the path which I prescribe to would only be applicable to the less-than 1% of the world population who are in ½ of their ways similar to me as the authority.

See then, of what value would this work be to the remaining 99%? Certainly there would be very little to no value. For this cause, I have constructed the Pinnacle of Purpose principally by the following designation and fundamental requirement – the Pinnacle of Purpose must be a high-level, universal model which dedicatedly accounts for the most common traits of man and speaks to the most applicable principles inherent to life itself.

Next I would state that each singular application of this guide will be unique for each seeker, for the dedicated principles of purpose result in countless manifestations contingent to the unique makeup of the individual. Thus as you would expect, our individual quests for fulfillment are dissimilar from an outward perspective even so the nature of the experience is intrinsically the same.

All the same, this current line of thought speaks to the relevance of this work as it pertains to its contents. Simultaneously there is tremendous relevance in its timeliness, for the message of fulfillment is always the message of the hour due to the infinite value of life.

Accordingly, it is not only imperative for each of us to embark on this transcending quest. It is also urgent, for the most opportune time to find fulfillment in life is always now due to the short-term and unpredictable natures of our existence.

As a matter of fact, the origin of this compilation is a memorandum I wrote years ago entitled, *"The Candle Document."* This document speaks at length to the ever-present urgency of man's subsistence in this present life, an urgency contingent to the ubiquitous reality that we (although alive and assuredly well this day) have no guarantees for tomorrow. Like a candle we all appear to burn unceasingly. Then suddenly our light goes out.

The problem is we generally don't know when our appointed time will be. Yet we know death is coming, looming around the corner, standing afar off in the distance, beckoning us to come along. Sans we, reluctant though we were, hemmed in as we were, slowly but surely make our way towards the inevitable conclusion of life as all who have gone before us. Alas, our candle too will one day be put out as we go the way of all the earth, and we too shall not return.

Sure we can ignore this reality. A great many of us do, seizing each day with a fictitious sense of invincibility while fatally embracing overconfidence and a lack of appreciation for all the variables of life; particularly those which are above us, those which are greater than us.

Then again, we can become disillusioned by the certain yet grim truth and find ourselves apathetic towards life while treating this most precious of gifts in an uninformed, nonchalant manner. As one philosophy puts it – today let us eat and drink, for tomorrow we shall die.

As for me, I would never encourage anyone to dwell on a daunting reality; neither would I have anyone become a hopeless victim to the common fate of men. Life is what it is – a bridge which ultimately leads man to his bereavement and, along this temporal crossing and prior to his own departure, he is persistently bereaved.

Does this reality do anything less than increase the pressing nature of one's dedication to the path of fulfillment? I think not. Therefore, we should all accept our impending fate and make the most out of the life we have been given, with sane urgency, and always bearing in mind that we have very few guarantees in life – and none of these are associated with the time of our sojourning here on earth.

The final word on life then is simply this – make the most of it. Don't wait for what you presume may be a more convenient season to begin taking this serious matter (that is your life) seriously. The time is now. Fulfillment is yours for the taking. The only question is – do you really want it?

I implore you to keep reading if you do, for I will lay out a clear path for you to find the fulfillment you seek within the following pages. Then it will be up to you to dedicate yourself to this path; fighting some days, struggling through others, pressing through most and overcoming all.

Then at long last you will have it, the ultimate prize of life and the greatest possession worth sharing – undying fulfillment indicated by a life decorated with the unremitting brilliance of unfeigned purpose, and an undying hope which allows you to transcend every life matter. Shall we begin?

INTRODUCTION

The World's Greatest Mystery

*

"I buried me and then I met, disastrous chaos, thus beset; I came
to know tis what you get, when to yourself you owe this debt."

THE ANSWER IS YOU

Do you know what the world's greatest mystery is? No; it's not the
Pyramids, Stonehenge, Area 51, or cafeteria meatloaf. The world's greatest
mystery is you. That's right – you. Regardless of what anyone says or thinks,
you are the world's best kept secret. The answer is you.

Now it is worth mentioning that you didn't start out this way. That
is to say, you were not always a mystery. At birth you inherited a clean
slate which clearly identified your destiny in life. Twas a perfect blend of
dreams, desires, and purpose at the forefront of your soul all waiting to
be expressed.

Nevertheless, as straightforward as this progression is, many of us will
never see this evolutionary expression; for whether it is in our own life or in
the life of one of the many individuals we know, this authentic manifestation
of the soul will never transpire. Thus regardless of the obvious nature of
our destiny, many of us will never find it. Be it disenchantment, chronic

cynicism, or excess distractions, many diverse factors will cause for our clear conduit to fulfillment to morph into a complex network of conflicting purposes and broken paths. To put it quite plainly — in time things changed. They always do.

Certainly there is a great deal I could say regarding this untimely change. Yet to sum it up in 2 words, I would simply state that *you changed*; specifically when you began the figurative yet inaccurate process of *growing up*.

Believe you me, growing up is not what it's all cooked up to be. Why not? Quite simply it's because growing up has unfortunately relapsed into a defective process in which many of us are actually *growing away* from our destiny. This ill-fated departure transpires as we are adversely influenced by family members, so-called friends, and the world at large.

It's a tragic disappearing act to say the least; the end results of which are always devastating, for the combination of these adverse influences causes for our initial blend of dreams and purpose to be buried beneath conflicting factors such as expectations, individuality, and control. Inopportunely these opposing factors work to perpetuate immense personal disillusionment; hence the great mystery of you.

Not convinced yet? How many times have you asked yourself, "Why did I do that?" Or how many times have you looked back on a poor decision you made and shook your head as you wondered, "What was I thinking?"

If you're like me, you've asked these questions more times than you can easily count. See our realities are sure. We only know ourselves in part for a good portion of our early lives. Due to a steady inundation of contradictory influences, we will find ourselves investing a great deal of energy and time in sifting through a great many ambitions, intentions, and the like.

The problem is many of these motivations are not in line with our destiny. Consequently our decisions in life will be heavily influenced by factors which do not reflect who we really are, factors which will fail to transform us into the person we were originally designed to be.

Now you are not just a mystery. You are no longer you. You, my friend, are an imposter. Many of us are or have been.

2 PATHS TO TAKE

Have I gotten your attention? If so, you are probably asking yourself questions like "what should I do" and "where should I go from here?" Classically there are only 2 paths to be taken at this juncture (which in my estimation is the most crucial crossroad in life).

Now the first path is an unfruitful attempt to go through life in the afore-described model of the self-impostor. Chances are you may very well find your destiny in the end and after all. However, in the off-chance this does occur, the path you take will be filled with missed opportunities, meager levels of contentment, and several regrets.

Moreover, these several disappointments may cause you to deviate from all worthwhile pursuits altogether and settle for an existence void of self-actualization (self-actualization being the activation of your full potential).

As for the second path, it is the good path. I know because I've followed this path as well as others who I've personally mentored, and yet others all over the world who are just like us. On this path you will embark upon an internal quest to sift through your personal minutia to differentiate your truest purposes in life from your secondary goals.

You will also address all those ambitions which you've somehow acquired yet do not correspond to your destiny whatsoever. We generally refer to these unfulfilling ends as "baggage" or "dead weight." Customarily they are some of the greatest deterrents to finding fulfillment. Hence they are factors you must deal with in your quest and you will.

Not only these; but you must eventually overcome all things to fulfill your destiny. All you have to do is follow the guidelines associated with the Pinnacle of Purpose, a combination of 7 unique steps which will not only unlock the "mystery of you." In dedicated fashion, the 7 levels of purpose will progressively transform you into the person you were originally destined to be from your beginning.

THE PINNACLE OF PURPOSE

Now although I utilize the model of a pinnacle to illustrate the 7 levels of purpose, the most accurate portrayal of your actual quest is a path – and as the conclusion of this path is fulfillment, I will regularly refer to this passageway as the *path to fulfillment*.

> **Every true purpose in your life is aligned with your destiny and propels you towards this decisive station.**

Moreover, seeing as you are able to increase your levels of fulfillment as you are in pursuit of your destiny, I will also refer to this crossing as the *path of fulfillment*. This brings out a crucial relationship between purpose, fulfillment, and destiny which I will offer as an interest point.

In line with this interest point, your personal progressive realization of your destiny is confirmed by your increasing levels of fulfillment. For this cause, your quest for fulfillment will be thoroughly depicted by a series of singular quests for purpose. Accordingly, there is no fulfillment in life without purpose just as there is no true purpose in your life unrelated to your destiny.

Going further, the Pinnacle of Purpose does more than assist each seeker in identifying their purposes in life. It also speaks to the most critical principles involved in achieving these purposes. As a matter of fact, approximately 80% of this illustration speaks to the model of self-actualization (i.e. the fulfillment of your purpose) while the remaining 20% speaks to the model of self-realization (i.e. the recognition of your purpose). This brings us to another interest point.

> *Walking any particular path is of greater value than simply knowing the path exists.*

We know this because the initiation of any journey of magnitude is predicated by a critical choice marked by extended deliberation and care. Subsequently, your decision to walk the path to fulfillment is preceded by your personal conclusion that succeeding this path is not only necessary; it is the most important thing you will ever do.

However, coming to this pivotal conclusion has very little value if you do not act upon it. In other words, you can't just talk about your destiny as if it is some far-off place you can not reach or some foreign concept you can not comprehend. Your destiny is within you. More perfectly, your destiny is the fulfillment of you.

Therefore, if you are determined to live a life of purpose, at some point you will have to throw your hat into the ring and be willing to get your hands dirty. Here's why – the enduring value of fulfillment is not realized by your knowledge of the path. It is realized as you walk the path.

If this is a conclusion you've come to and a path you are prepared to travel, I ask you to consider the following model [See image: Pinnacle of Purpose].

Pinnacle of Purpose

As you can plainly see, there is nothing revolutionary about this model whatsoever. Not only is it simple; it is (as I mentioned early on) in concert with some of the more fundamental characteristics of man.

Nevertheless, there is something revolutionary about walking the path and progressively applying each degree of purpose in your life; for as you unlock each degree of purpose, you will experience an amazing metamorphosis which continues as you walk the path to fulfillment until you become one with your destiny. Not only is this something to be accounted for; it is a matter which transcends every other cause you could dedicate your life to.

WALKING THE PATH

It goes without saying that this particular transformation is as awesome as it is breathtaking. This is true even though it will not always feel awesome as you are on your personal journey, for there will be various difficult stretches of travel highlighted by adverse weather so to speak. Yet this is something we should all be encouraged by, for even a plant needs both rain and sun to grow. How then shall we come naturally into a state of fulfillment following any other model?

> **If your focus is exclusively on fulfillment, you will be unable to relate all the challenges on your quest to the ultimate prize.**

This speaks to the greatest caution I would offer to each purpose seeker and the final word to be given prior to initiating our decisive series of lectures. The caution – even though fulfillment is the ultimate goal of our quest, it can not be our primary focus while we are in the midst of our journey. The reason why represents another interest point.

As a result of this letdown, many will become disoriented regarding their path and fatally get off track. As they fail to see the connection between their struggles and their goals, they will eventually reach their breaking point and settle as so many have done before them, and as so many will do after. The question is – what will you do?

I trust you are up for the challenge and are determined to fulfill your purpose at all costs. If this is so, then you must learn to embrace all the challenges on your path, seeing you will be unable to succeed any other way.

Then again, I call you to remember that you can not outrun troubles. Neither can you hide from them; especially if you are intent on finding fulfillment. My dear friends, in order to have that which you seek, you must overcome everything which stands in your way and there is no other way.

So arise, and conquer; for every time you overcome any obstacle in your quest, you effectually become stronger. So don't consider who you are now and stumble in fear of those things which you perceive you are unable to do. Instead consider who you shall be at the conclusion of your quest and ascend to take hold of the future you believe you are able to have.

Finally you must never forget this – the quest for fulfillment is not singly about the eventual attainment of the prize. No my friends; the quest for fulfillment is about learning something new every day and being enriched by the totality of the journey, for it is the journey which allows you to discover your purpose while finding fulfillment. It is the journey which allows you to unlock your personal mystery, and it is the journey which daily transforms you into a man or a woman fit for their destiny.

So remain focused on the evolution of the journey and the daily objectives of your quest. Only then will you find it and forever you will have, at long last, your destiny. It's waiting for you. The only question is – are you ready for it?

CHAPTER 1

For Once It's All About You

*

"I close my eyes and this I see, a perfect life where I am free;
To be whatever I want to be, for those I love, yet more for me."

I DID IT ON PURPOSE

"I didn't do it on purpose" was one of my favorite sayings as a child. Why? It is because this confession had gotten me out of trouble on possibly 1,000 occasions, a minor exaggeration to be sure. In any event, these 6 words were priceless because they constituted my original "get out of jail free card" and saved me in several sticky situations.

Now this card didn't work all the time, mind you. After all, there were some things I did which I could neither honestly nor semi-honestly justify with my patented excuse, and I wasn't going to compromise the longevity of my lucky card for any incident which was clearly inexcusable. No sir; I was going to drink from this well until the water ran dry – which it did and much sooner than I would have liked. Alas, all good things must come to an end.

Fast-forward several years in time. Here you'll find me with a much different outlook on life and a new preferred saying. That would be, *"I did it on purpose,"* a definitive statement which speaks to one of the most profound realities in life. As such, I will offer it as an interest point.

> **Whether good or evil, everything we do is in effect on purpose, for every life matter is tied to a choice and every choice we make is tied to a purpose.**

Classically this is where the rubber meets the road; for as everything we do is incontestably on purpose, our consistent actions reveal who we are with regards to our inner self as opposed to our personal face-value. Accordingly, it is our actions more so than our words which tell the tale of the man or woman we're trying to be.

Notwithstanding, this tale does not always reflect who we *truly* are. In this regard, some of us at face-value are pretenders who are trying to be someone they're not. This is why establishing our life upon a firm foundation of purpose is so vital, for the consistent inundation of purpose ensures our intentions and consequent actions are perfectly aligned with our destiny. Therefore, the first step in unlocking your personal mystery is dedicating yourself to being yourself and living a life of purpose.

TRUE YOU

Now if you're like me, you know very few people who consistently say what they mean and mean what they say. You know even fewer people who without fail practice what they preach. Why the inconsistency? For the most part it's because their lives are established on conflicting purposes; hence the irregularity.

Then again if you're like me, you may have noticed this contradictory trend a time or two in your own life. So what did you do? I'll tell you what

I did – I set out on a personal journey to discover a path where everything I did was not only *on purpose*, but *with purpose*; specifically purposes which reflected "the real me."

Who am I referring to when I mention *the real me*? Definitively I am referring to the man I would turn out to be after I successfully established my purpose in life. That is the man I was destined to become before various conflicting factors set me off-course and led me down paths contrary to my destiny. Consequently, if there is a real me, there must be a version of me who is not as real.

I'll never forget the first time I heard someone teach on the concept of *true north*. It was during an astronomy lecture at Ball State University. I remember thinking to myself, "If there is a true north, then what is the *regular north* I've been learning since kindergarten?"

Of course everything made more sense at the end of the lecture. Without going into the details, there are multiple manifestations of the astronomical concept of north. However, only one of these manifestations is true north; that is the direction along the earth's surface towards the geographic North Pole. The other variations may at times be congruent and persistently similar. Yet they are not consistently the same as true north.

The same rule applies to all of us. See the majority of us exhibit multiple manifestations. The two prevailing manifestations are "you now" and "true you." *You now* is the person you are at this present moment. *True you* is the person you will become once all of your singular purposes are properly aligned and consequently coherent. Accordingly, the search for purpose in life is actually a search for the most authentic version of you. It's the elongated process in which you discover and are converted into true you.

STRENGTH IN DIVERSITY

The next question we must attend to is this – why is it important for us to be true to ourselves? Honestly I could provide over 100 reasons why this cause is beyond essential. However, I would like to focus on 1 in particular; that is diversity.

Certainly diversity is a prominent pillar of every progressive society. For an example consider a football team and ask yourself this question – how effective would a team be if everyone on the offense was a quarterback and everyone on the defense was a linebacker? Trust me; not only would this team be unsuccessful. They wouldn't be very enjoyable to watch (unless perhaps you were rooting for the opposing team).

Therefore, I would ask you to consider this follow-up question – if everyone in your society (e.g. business unit, family or organization) were a carbon copy of the person next to them, how successful would your society be? Think about it.

Here's the next point I would like to make – every progressive society is depicted by roles which are fulfilled by the successful administration of an over-arching, correlating assignment (which I will consciously refer to as an office throughout this composition). A principal key to the success of each society, then, is that each office is occupied by the person best suited to fulfill its corresponding roles. In every other case, the inclusive lack from a poor arrangement will prevent the society from reaching its full potential. As such, it would continually degenerate until corrective actions are taken.

Almost 10 years ago I was the Director of Consulting Services at one of the largest IT firms based out of Indiana. There I enjoyed managing one of my favorite and most successful teams. It was also one of my most diverse teams, a crucial factor which positioned us to incur awesome measures of success; more success than we would have achieved otherwise.

Upon understanding this development, I began actively looking for ways to increase the diversity of our team. Thus whenever I interviewed potential candidates to fill open positions, I first considered the members currently on the team. Then I not only looked for the candidate who exceeded my expectations; I also looked for someone who would add diversity to our group.

Masterfully my strategy proved correct every time the team grew. By gradually increasing the diversity of our team, we found ourselves consistently innovated with new ideas, processes, and ways of thinking in general.

Sure we had a pretty large group of seasoned professionals who possessed awesome talents and the ability to get a lot done. However, the greatest source of our strength was not our numbers or our expertise. It was our diversity and the awesome opportunities it presented us.

THE WORLD NEEDS YOU

At the same time, I learned that managing and participating in a diverse group presents several challenges. In particular, it forces each team member to regularly rethink and often recalibrate their views. These actions (though very necessary) are sometimes difficult because many of us have a hard time considering or admitting when we are wrong or when our way of doing things is not necessarily the best way to get things done.

Fortunately there was no one in our group who was too terribly rigid that they couldn't see past their own methodologies. Hence this is not where I encountered most of my challenges. These unforeseen happenstances transpired as a result of the inverse scenario; explicitly some team members became discouraged when their ideas were not adopted by the group and began to withdraw.

Consensus is my preferred way to lead and always has been. So I recognized I was indirectly responsible for the withdrawal that was occurring. In consequence, I had to upgrade my management strategy to account for this unanticipated offshoot.

In time I came up with the perfect solution. I met individually with those who were withdrawn from the group and reassured them that they were critical to the team's success. More importantly I told them why. In doing so, I reminded them why I hired them and described future scenarios where I was confident their expertise and background would be crucial to the team's continued success.

The lesson I learned then was sure – there are peaks and valleys in everyone's life. For that reason, we can not allow for the valleys to cause us to lose sight of the value of our role as it pertains to the group's success. Neither can we allow the peaks to deceive us into believing we're "all that," for no one person will ever exceed the value and potential of a progressive group or society.

What it all comes down to is this – the world needs you. You don't have to take my word for it. Just consider all of your offices in life and ask yourself this question – who is better suited to fulfill each of my offices than me?

See I'm convinced the vast majority of us have at least one life office which no one can fulfill better than we can. For those of you who are unconvinced, this does not mean the world doesn't need you. Quite the contrary; what the world needs is for you to find a way to succeed in the offices you were called to and in the roles you were destined to fulfill.

Now the cause behind this need is certain and one which I hope you

> **The only person who can successfully fulfill your purpose is you.**

will never forget. Therefore I will offer it as an interest point.

This matter lends itself to why societies degenerate. It is because critical roles are not being fulfilled by the person best suited to fulfill them. Consequently, the correlating offices are either empty or occupied by someone less qualified – and alas, everyone involved will suffer the consequences in the end and after all.

BE YOURSELF

"Everybody has an office," I declared to an adult group to whom I was delivering a spiritual lecture. "The problem," I told them, "is that many fail to recognize their purpose in life because they are fatally trying to be someone they're not."

Then I shared with them a profound statement which I will offer as

> **Be yourself or "you" will die.**

another interest point.

Understandably *death* in this context is not literal. It is figurative. That is to say, the longer you try to be someone you're not, the farther you will migrate away from your true self.

Stay on this path long enough and you will be so far removed from your true self that he or she will be metaphorically deceased – and as it is scarcely possible, we all perceive the likelihood of raising someone from the dead (metaphorically or literally).

Now I was able to make this decisive declaration for one simple cause – I had been there. Admittedly, I knew what it was like to lose sight of my true self because I was too busy trying to be someone who I thought was better than me; namely someone who I thought the world would better appreciate.

That's when I realized I had effectually become a self-contradiction. By trying to be someone I was not, I was contradicting my own existence as well as decreasing my personal value.

While on this regressive road, I began to understand the nature of our world and found it to be similar to that of a spoiled child. You know the type. You've seen them throwing themselves out in grocery stores and acting unruly in restaurants all across the country. The $500 question is simply *why?*

Here's the answer – a spoiled child doesn't really know what they want. Consequently, the worst thing for them is a parent who constantly bends over backwards to meet their child's unrealistic and unfounded demands, for these actions only work to reinforce the deficits of the child. This is true even though the parent is merely trying to be appreciated by giving the child what they presume he or she wants.

What these parents fail to realize is tragically classic; that is the child does not know what he or she wants. This is precisely why they are often only able to appreciate one thing; that is a parent who will stop spoiling them and teach them the true meaning of appreciation.

Trust me; it's bad business when you have parents trying to befriend a child, for every parent should focus first and foremost on being a credible authority as this is the first step in effectively raising children. This is especially the case during their informative years.

How does this example relate to you and the world? Well I'll tell you. The world is like a spoiled child in that it is by default inappreciative. Consequently, it will never appreciate those who bend over backwards trying to be someone they presume everyone will accept. On the contrary, the only way the world will appreciate you is if you stop trying to be everyone's friend and start being yourself.

Again I ask you to trust me and faithfully consider the following statement – being yourself is the only thing you'll ever truly be good at. This truism speaks to another interest point.

> **The world can not appreciate you if you do not first appreciate yourself.**

On this wise, the one sure way to tell if you appreciate yourself is by determining how committed you are to being yourself. Or as the young people tell it, "Just do you."

Certainly this is the only way you will ever unlock your personal mystery because again, as the young people say, you are "keeping it real." In essence, you are being yourself in every situation. This allows people to know what to expect out of you regardless of the situation or circumstances you are in.

Markedly this is exactly when the world will begin to appreciate you, for you will have proven yourself to be reliable – and who doesn't appreciate someone who they can consistently count on?

All the same, as wonderful as this occasion is, enduring appreciation does not come painlessly. Neither does it come quickly. Contrasting, it comes tenderly and gradually. The same way a small child does not instantly appreciate the discipline of a wise parent, the world will not immediately appreciate the value of an authentic man or woman.

Do not be troubled by this reality, for in time this value will surely be realized. You just have to be committed to standing up for yourself even when you're standing alone – and there will be several instances when you are.

ARE YOU READY TO WALK THE PATH?

How does this all relate to living a life of purpose? Decisively everything we have discussed thus far is only possible if we have effectively established our unique purposes in life. In this regard, your life purposes (i.e. the distinct causes which collective constitute your purpose) are like tour guides. Their job is to guide you along the path which leads to your destiny.

As for me, I've walked this path in my life and have achieved awesome levels of fulfillment and success. From now, I want to share what I have learned by leaving behind breadcrumbs for others to follow. Therefore, the following pages of this book will speak to the aforementioned path of fulfillment and provide various life examples for both validation and understanding.

All things considered, everything in life is a choice (with the lone exception of physiological involuntary actions). Thus conclusively, if you choose to follow this path, I can make you the following guarantee – even though you will endure various seasons of grind and change, you will eventually acquire the greatest measures of fulfillment and success the world has to offer. That's my personal guarantee.

So if this pledge sounds like a good deal to you, keep reading this book. I'm going to show you how I got there and how you can get there too.

On the other hand, if you decide not to follow this path or some similar path, I can guarantee you the opposite. Regrettably you will fail to acquire the greatest measures of fulfillment and success while never realizing your true potential. Furthermore, you will still endure various seasons of grind and change.

Granted this is not the classic life-or-death scenario; not even close. However, the quality of your life is at stake. Thus the question of the hour is simply this – how much fulfillment and success are you prepared to leave on the table?

THE SUMMATION

The majority of us will reach a point in our lives where we discover that we are not authentic reflections of the man or woman inside. As an ill-advised traveler, we've deviated from the beaten path and gotten lost.

All the same, course correction is not a difficult matter. All we need is a map. Enter: the Pinnacle of Purpose, a dedicated roadmap which provides purposeful direction along the path which leads to true you and concludes with the greatest allotment of fulfillment and success this life can afford.

What is more, the Pinnacle of Purpose (as illustrated in this composition) provides ample instructions and advice on how to handle various situations which could potentially cause us to lose our way. This manner of intelligence is critical because our world is unfortunately filled with haters and doubters. Disappointingly these losers in life are going to invest time in throwing stones at us as we carry on our quest.

Now in submitting this warning, I would advise each reader not to be overly concerned about this matter. See I'm not only going to show you how to become immune to these unwarranted acts. I'm also going to show you how to use these stones to help you get to where you are going. Advantageously I'm going to show you how to turn their throwing stones into your stepping stones.

Last but surely not least, I'm going to lay a foundation for achieving self-actualization by discussing the importance of excelling in each of our life offices – and although the full disclosure of this process will be addressed in the next composition in this series, it is imperative for each purpose seeker to understand how important it is to always give our best effort in every life situation. For once we establish this model way of living, and everything else will begin to seamlessly fall into place. This brings me to my final world on this lecture.

> **No matter what anyone tells you, the world needs you. Therefore, if you don't know who you are, it's time you found out. Only then will you be truly appreciated and wholly succeed in those offices you were called to fulfill.**

_____

CHAPTER 2

Destiny and Fate

*

*"In stumbling through my life and free, I found that
I was forced to breathe; And meet what fate had
planned for me, until I found my destiny."*

VICTIMS AND BENEFACTORS

The next matter I would like to discuss concerning the Pinnacle of Purpose is its over-arching objective. That would be to strategically align each of us with our destiny.

Obviously destiny is not an uncommon concept. Yet I am not convinced it is consistently considered in its purest form; explicitly a form applicable to the foundational model of purpose. Thus I will provide an appropriate definition of this crucial term.

Destiny is the pre-appointed collection of life purposes one is designed to achieve contingent to a vast array of inherited and naturally acquired strengths, gifts, and personality traits, all of which are designated for the successful fulfillment of each purpose.

Harmonizing this rendering of destiny with our model of fulfillment, I would submit the following statement – we will find very little fulfillment in our lives outside of the path which leads to our destiny.

Now the primary source of this reality is fate. Although often used interchangeably, destiny and fate are very dissimilar for numerous reasons. Therefore, I will provide an applicable definition for fate with specific regards to our model of purpose.

Fate represents any unavoidable occasion in life (good or bad) which we must endure.

Contrasting these 2 concepts and observing life in general, I have arrived at the following conclusion – fate, more often than not, works against our destiny. This is clearly seen by observing the more distressing turns of fate, for these make traveling the path to fulfillment increasingly difficult.

At the same time, they are the inevitable derivatives of the reality that we live in an imperfect world filled with imperfect people. As a consequence, offences are going to come. Bad things are going to happen to good people, and life is going to provide each of us with our fair share of disappointment and tragedy. It is the corporate fate of all men.

Nevertheless, we don't have to let fate prevent us from reaching our destiny. I would go as far as to say *we can't,* for fulfilling our destiny is the apex of progressive living. Thus all who fail to fulfill their destiny will fatefully go through life enduring reckonable measures of suffering and pain, all of which can be dissolved by the dedicated application of purpose.

I would at this time ask you to consider the violence and crime in our world and ask yourself this question – were the perpetrators experiencing awesome levels of fulfillment when they committed these crimes? Were they living their lives with purpose or had they truly dedicated themselves to this righteous cause? Reason within yourselves what the answer to this inquiry should be.

As for me, I find a certain level of uneasiness and disquieting for even having to ask; but I do know this – there are ultimately 2 kinds of people in our world. There are those who will become victims of fate and those who will become benefactors by fulfilling their unique destiny. The question I have for each reader is simply this – which will you be?

ARCHITECTS OF FATE

Personally I would advise you to choose the path of the benefactor, for a choice in favor of your destiny is always the best choice. Notwithstanding, you still have to deal with the various channels of fate. On this wise, the only manner to avoid falling quarry to fate is by becoming an architect. That is to say, you must learn how to effectively manage all the unforeseen occasions in your life and employ them towards your personal quest for fulfillment.

Now I borrow this analogy from a poem entitled, *"The Builders"* authored by the literary genius of one, Henry Wadsworth Longfellow. It reads as follows:

"The Builders," by Henry Wadsworth Longfellow (1807-1882)

All are architects of Fate, Working in these walls of Time; Some with massive deeds and great, Some with ornaments of rhyme.

Nothing useless is, or low; Each thing in its place is best; And what seems but idle show strengthens and supports the rest.

For the structure that we raise, Time is with materials filled; Our to-days and yesterdays are the blocks with which we build.

Truly shape and fashion these; Leave no yawning gaps between;
Think not, because no man sees, Such things will remain unseen.

In the elder days of Art, Builders wrought with greatest care
Each minute and unseen part; For the Gods see everywhere.

Let us do our work as well, Both the unseen and the seen; Make
the house, where Gods may dwell, Beautiful, entire, and clean.

Else our lives are incomplete, Standing in these walls of Time,
Broken stairways, where the feet stumble as they seek to climb.

Build to-day, then, strong and sure, With a firm and ample
base; And ascending and secure shall to-morrow find its place.

Thus alone can we attain to those turrets, where the eye Sees
the world as one vast plain, and one boundless reach of sky.

A simply remarkable poem, I'd say, and one which wholly captures the essence of our pursuit of destiny. In this order, and due to the endless channels of fate, our quest will not be a cake-walk. On the contrary, life is going to yield both soil and gravel for us to grow our gardens. It will provide us with both stone and debris to build our homes.

Therefore, my goal is to help each purpose seeker become a master builder. My purpose is to spur on your transformation into a dedicated architect who will be considered as a draftsman of renown in generations to come.

See you are not going to look at the seemingly useless and vexing offshoots of fate and become discouraged; not you. You, my friend, are going to gain the power to absorb each negative occasion and the discernment to determine how you can use each to your advantage.

BE AN OPPORTUNIST AND SAVE THE CAUSE

As the man in another remarkable poem composed by Edward Rowland Sill entitled, *"Opportunity"* [See Appendix A], you are going to win a great victory with the symbolical equivalence of a broken sword. In awesome fashion, you are going to fulfill your destiny in spite of the many difficult turns of fate.

This truth reveals a crucial aspect concerning your quest for fulfillment; unmistakably, it's not what you have in your hand which matters most. It's what you have in your heart which counts, for you have little to no control of what is truly in your hands. Therefore, if you base your levels of commitment and determination upon this relative unknown, it will be impossible to gauge your actions. They will be as inconsistent as your physical circumstances are unpredictable.

As a result, you will (over time) fail to stay the course; for when your physical circumstances change, your levels of commitment and determination will also change.

Moreover, since the trending nature of fate in our world is undeniably negative, this change is usually going to be for the worse. In view of that, we must look to our hearts if we are to fulfill our destinies; for unlike our circumstances, we can effectively dictate the landscape of our hearts so long as we have purpose.

This speaks to the valor of the man in this epic poem who wrought a great victory with a broken sword. Unlike the other warriors who persisted at the latter stages of this battle, he didn't have very much to work with (physically that is). Yet he had a purpose, and a relentless desire to see his destiny fulfilled.

See he was the king's son. Accordingly, his kingdom and his legacy were at stake. The same goes for each of us, for every family is a kingdom and every life emits a legacy.

Now step back a few frames in this particular battle. Here we will find the original possessor of this broken sword. Unfortunately he didn't share the sentiments of our hero. On the contrary, he reasoned within himself, *"Had I a sword of keener steel—that blue blade that the king's son bears, — but this blunt thing—!"* Alas, in utter disillusionment, he snapped and flung it from his hand, and lowering crept away and left the field.

As I said before, there are 2 men we can choose to be in life. We can be the man who snapped because he was more focused on what he didn't have (i.e. his circumstances). Or we can be the man who was so desperate to fulfill his destiny that he defied all odds and saved a great cause that heroic day. My advice to each purpose seeker is simply this – be an opportunist and save the cause.

ALL ROADS LEAD TO DESTINY

Moving on, for all the reasons and cases I have prior offered, it should be clear that we were all originally destined to experience fulfillment at our birth. Whether we are a king's son or the son of a lowly carpenter, we all have a destiny to fulfill – and the value of each singular fulfillment is the same even so the physical manifestation is distinctly unique.

Another significant matter reveals we all initiate our ascent of the Pinnacle of Purpose from different positions. Accordingly, it is inaccurate to state that there is only one way to ascend to the top of this mountain. On the contrary, there are multiple routes you can take to align yourself with and ultimately reach your destiny. However, they all follow the same principles beginning with confidence and concluding with peace.

All things considered, the fact that there are multiples ways to go about reaching our destiny is good news for everyone, for it assures us that there will always be a way for us to get back onto the path which leads to our destiny if we should stray.

Sure getting back on track is not the ideal scenario. Yet since none of us are born into perfection, it is comforting to know that we will be able to recover from any mistake or miscalculation we may perchance make.

Besides this, there is another matter which is certain on this wise; that is every road within the Pinnacle of Purpose leads upwards. Accordingly, your decision to follow after your destiny will always be the progressive choice.

Then again it will always be clear, for traveling upwards will always require more exertion than descending downwards. For this cause, rising to fulfill your destiny will always be more demanding than succumbing to the oft harsh realities of fate.

DESIGNED FOR DESTINY

I would at this time pose a question to each reader – what is the first word that comes to your mind when you consider the word *destiny*? The first word that comes to my mind is *destined*, a model which insinuates something was made for a particular purpose.

Applying this definition to our line of discussion, we are all uniquely designed to achieve a specific set of purposes in our lives – and these purposes, if successfully fulfilled, will bring us to our destiny.

Now some of these purposes are easy to determine. For example, most women are naturally destined to be wives, mothers, and eventually grandmothers. All they have to do is follow the progressive ways of the world and they will more than likely find themselves in one or all of these offices at some point or another.

On the other hand, some of our purposes in life are not so straightforward. For another example consider a young woman who excels in the areas of math and science. Clearly there are various careers she could be successful in. Thus determining the field which will provide her with the greatest measures of fulfillment and success will not likely be as simple as deciding whether or not she will marry.

Furthermore, deciding a career is by and large the apex of our destiny. This is because we will spend the vast majority of our lives operating in a professional office. Accordingly, the decision-making process involved with determining our career is often the most crucial.

Nonetheless, this doesn't take away from the other facets of our destiny. Our roles as parents, spouses, and members of any progressive society are just as critical. The only difference is we will spend much more dedicated time in our professions than our predominately social offices. Still the tie that binds is this – we were designed to fulfill them all, and we must if we are to live a life of purpose.

CAN YOU KEEP IT REAL?

Going further, we must be cognizant of the evolution of our life offices. In this order, we must realize that our destiny is a collection of our current life purposes and those designated for our future. As such, our life purposes are contingent to our personal evolution and will evolve as we evolve.

For example, the destiny of one man could include the following offices: a son, a brother, a father, a grandfather, a business man, a pastor, a counselor, and a domestic violence advocate. All the same, this particular man would not initially be a son and a father at the same time. True, he will eventually become a father; yet this will not transpire until a much later season in his life.

In accordance with this reality, we must always keep in mind that our destiny is progressive. Therefore, we must be willing to make all the necessary changes in our lives to make sure we are at all times in line with it. This is what it means to keep it real.

Here again, this is important because there is a pretender within all of us who doesn't want to line up with our destiny. The reasons why are endless, and they all have to do with some inner reluctance to endure the inevitable seasons of change in our lives. Subsequently, as our path to fulfillment is evolutionary, those who are adverse to change are not going to fare well until they resolve their corresponding fears.

In light of this truth, this message clearly is not just for young people who are at the cusp of adulthood and experiencing the greatest measure of change with regards to their destiny. This message is for everyone, including those who already have a pretty good hold on their life offices.

I can state this with certainty for a sure cause – the moment we start feeling comfortable in life, we will find our destiny taking an unexpected turn while forcing us to endure various seasons of change. So here's the question of the hour regarding your destiny and the path to fulfillment – can you follow the path no matter how many twists, turns, and unexpected occasions it presents you with?

Here's a follow-up question – when times are changing in the most difficult and sudden ways, and while others are flailing and reverting to their fraudulent nature, can you keep it real?

THE SUMMATION

Although we are all fitly designed for our destiny, fulfilling it will not be easy. This is in large part due to the difficult, often erratic turns of fate. These turns are the inescapable derivatives of our existence in a complex and generally troubled world. Therefore, as we are certainly unable to avoid the happenings of fate, we must learn how to deal with each contrary occasion effectively. Less we find ourselves victims of fate as opposed to architects of renown.

Notwithstanding, not every channel of fate is negative. There are in fact positive turns. We generally refer to these as *luck* or *good fortune*. Yet consider how many times you have heard someone say, "It's my lucky day." Really think about it.

If you're like me, you've heard this declaration a lot less frequently than you've heard someone complaining about some negative, unanticipated occurrence in their life — and if you did perchance hear someone testify to some unforeseen occasion of good fortune, you were probably very surprised. It's just the way life is.

No doubt this reality makes having a positive outlook invaluable; for as we know life is highlighted by the prevailing difficult turns of fate, we must always look on the "bright side" to ensure we make the most of each situation.

See even the negative turns carry opportunity. As the saying goes, every cloud has a silver lining. We just have to be willing to go the extra mile to find it. This brings me to my final word on destiny and fate.

You were designed for your destiny. Accordingly, every progressive road you take leads to this awesome station. All you have to do is discover your life purposes and they will point you in the right direction.

CHAPTER 3

Change

*

*"I'm holding on to understand, whatever was I'd
in my hands; Designs stretched way outside the
spanned, and never went the way I planned."*

THE GREAT HUMAN DILEMMA

Classically one of the few *certainties* in life is change, a concept I refer
to as the *"Great Human Dilemma"* or the *"Change Principle."* I refer to it as such
because change always results in conflict and people generally consider
conflict from a negative perspective. This causes them to miss out on one of
the most important aspects of conflict; that would be the fact that conflict
will always present us with multiple opportunities of both the positive and
negative variety. Accordingly, there is always the possibility that good could
come from conflict.

Here's the catch — we will have to deal with various stress factors to
cash in on the advanced opportunities which evolve from conflict, and the
greatest of these is change.

I was working with a new project team as a program manager for an
IT consulting firm years ago. During my first team meeting I strategically

asked the group whether or not they liked change, and was not surprised when no one said they did. I actually anticipated this response; yet I asked the question regardless because I wanted to prove a point.

See I was brought on to save this program from the corporate recycle bin and I fully intended to do so, for I had developed a distinguished reputation as a problem-solver and a fixer in those days in large part due to my change management skills. Since so many IT projects "go south" or in some way deviate from the original schedule and requirements, a program manager with the dexterity to effectively manage the endless avenues of change is worth their weight in gold.

Here's more food for thought – I've managed over 100 projects in my career, and amazingly I can count on 1 hand the number of projects I've managed to completion which had little to no deviations from the original plan. It's just the way things are in IT, for change is not an unexpected occasion in our world. Change is our reality.

Knowing this, I could succumb to the oft harsh reality of my professional trade; or I could refuse to be discouraged by the persistent reality of all IT professionals and become an architect of one of the most difficult turns of fate – change.

Decisively I chose the latter. Thus perceiving the nature of this particular corporate beast, I prepared myself to be assigned to projects which I already knew would deviate and tirelessly developed the skills set to manage them successfully – my secret weapon.

This speaks to my initial inquiry to my team. So why do you think they were not interested in change? After all, they had spent several months on failing projects which could potentially have a negative impact on their company and ultimately their careers. Realistically how were they going to turn things around apart from some manner of change? Is this not the modern rendering of insanity? Yet how many times do we repeat the same behaviors or stay in situations which are not changing and expect (or rather hope for) different results?

THE POWER OF PERSPECTIVE

Definitively the reason why my team was initially averse to change is because they held a poor perspective of change. Here's what they failed to realize – change always presents us with new prospects, and some of these are of the good variety.

However, because my team obviously had preconceived notions about change in any form, they were positioning themselves to miss out on a golden opportunity; that would be saving their project. In consequence, as they had failed to consider how their project could not improve apart from some degree of change, they had effectively closed the door on success.

This speaks to the power of perspective. Truly our perspective on any matter has the greatest net effect on our perception of that matter – and our perception is not only the most important thing; it is everything.

This is uniformly evident as it pertains to change; for as change is a constant reality as it pertains to our path to fulfillment, our inability to employ an applicable perspective of change will fatefully prevent us from fulfilling our purpose.

I would at this time put forth a question to each reader. Which of the following descriptions depicts you best – *glass half-empty* or *glass half-full*? If you're like me, most of the people you know prescribe to the "glass half-empty" model. What these fail to realize is that this pessimistic viewpoint is self-fulfilling; for if you're expecting the worst, the worst will come to pass simply because you were expecting it.

I can say this with certainty for the following cause – if you are expecting anything less than success, you will inadvertently (and likely subconsciously) gauge your efforts to correspond to your half-empty expectations. For this cause (and contrary to the beliefs of some), you're not going to get too much out of anything if you're not willing to adequately invest in it.

We know this because nearly everything we do in life (especially our achievements) begins with some measure of hope. Thus hope is our principal motivation for taking any action.

Consider the first young lady you ever asked out on a date, gentlemen, and ask yourself why you did it. I believe our answers would all be the same; quite simply we were hoping she would say *yes*. Or, if you were like me, you would have gladly settled for *maybe*.

Now flip the script. Think of a young lady who you were not so interested in. Did you ever ask her out? No, you didn't; simply because you, for whatever reason, didn't hope for it. Hence there was no motivation on your part to pursue her.

Classically this is how a glass half-empty perspective becomes self-fulfilling. It is because this poor perspective has little to no hope. Therefore, the same way you would not put forth any true effort to ask out someone you're not really interested in, you're not likely going to put forth the required effort to succeed in a situation which you have little confidence in. Unfortunately this is where I found my team at the beginning of my tenure.

So what do you think I did? Well I'll tell you. After they admitted they were not big fans of change, I asked them the following question – how many of you would like to turn this project around?

Predictably they all voted in the affirmative. So I then went on to ask several related questions for one reason – I wanted to get them excited about change before dropping the bomb on them, and that's exactly what I did. After everyone had talked about saving the project, having the opportunity of increased job security, taking their professional game to another level, etc., etc., etc., I told them something they probably didn't expect or want to hear. I said to them, "If this is truly what you all want, we're going to have to make some changes…"

CHANGE CAN DO YOU GOOD

Now most of us have no qualms with the opportunities associated with change. Our misgivings usually have to do with the general idea of change and making some measure of modification in our lives. This is true even though most of our lives are far from perfect, a semi-paradox which I attribute to 2 reasons:

1. **People often find comfort in the *"known"* even when the known is less than desirable.**
2. **People typically settle for the status quo because it is much easier to settle than it is to labor to the point of excellence.**

Characteristically the first reason is almost always a prelude to the second. It was definitely the case with my team. See even though the program was failing, they knew what to expect and found some degree of comfort in the aspect of *knowing*.

Besides this, they had become content with the low expectations on them because of their lack of productivity and subsequently began to settle for less than their best. This being the case, how could anyone deny the fact that a change could do this group some good?

Now in understanding their need for change, there were 2 critical steps I had to take to ensure this change would be implemented successfully. First of all, I had to get them to change their perspective. Else they would not be motivated to pursue the opportunities of change.

Strategically this is why I asked them so many questions; specifically questions which appealed to their personal objectives. They had to, for how can you convince anyone to do anything (especially adults) if they don't perceive a high level of value in their compliance? Trust me; it's an endeavor as close to impossible as any other.

For this very cause, one of my preferred sayings and a standard I live by suggests the following – to have a successful team, everybody has to get their bite of the apple (i.e. the second critical step in implementing change).

Think about it. When asked to do anything outside of our preferred manner of execution, we all want to know the answer to one very simple question. The question – what's in it for me?

Now some folks don't have a high asking price. Then again some folks do. Therefore, when you're looking to motivate others, my advice to you is simply this – make sure you have a big apple. This will allow you to meet everyone's asking price and hopefully you'll have some left over for a rainy day.

THE BIG APPLE

I anticipate the question most of you are asking at this time and will ask it in kind – how do I get the big apple? The answer lies solely in your ability to motivate. On this wise, your artistic abilities far outweigh your financial capacity because people, for the most part, are not purely motivated by money. They are motivated by opportunities.

Decisively opportunities are the primary vehicles of fulfillment while your personal search for meaning is the driver. This elevates the requisite of opportunity as the prevailing factor of motivation as it pertains to your quest, for it effectively bridges the gap between your life purposes and the ultimate goal of fulfillment.

Not only does this connection serve as a crucial validation of our life purposes; each opportunity figuratively lights our path. As a series of lanterns situated along the continuous corridors of self-actualization, opportunity (along with a positive perspective) ensures our path to fulfillment is always clear and bright.

I refer to this principle as the *"Treasure Principle."* Beyond providing a concise analysis of the power of opportunity, this principle also keys in on the heart; a crucial facet of our being because it is the location of our treasures in life. Accordingly, if we are to make the most of our opportunities, our heart has to be in it.

How does this relate to getting the big apple? Obviously the apple in this model is figurative, unless of course you're an apple farmer. Otherwise it's symbolic of a combination of all the opportunities and desires of the group you're working with. As their leader, your first task is to paint a picture in the mind of each team member which supersedes their realistic expectations for the initiatives they are assigned to and yet remains realistic. Surely this is a riddle and one you must solve at regular intervals in your quest.

Lo and behold that is exactly what I did. Even though I had a team of diverse individuals with diverse roles, I was able to effectively motivate each of them simply by appealing to their desires for the program and the awesome opportunities that would follow them if they were successful (both individually and collectively).

This is what it means to have a big apple. You have to paint a picture in the mind of each group member which allows them to visualize an apple big enough for everyone to get their fair share; specifically a share which they conclude is more than worth them putting forth their best effort.

As far as success goes, you're going to need each team member to put forth their best effort to be successful in any group endeavor. So if you want to be an effective leader and motivator, I'll say it once more – make sure you have a big apple.

THE MAN WITH THE PLAN

Now after you have successfully motivated your team with the big apple, you have to formulate a plan which can be communicated to your team at a high level. In this order, I have become accustomed to using a roadmap which has 2 distinct features: all the major milestones on your path to fulfillment and a clear explanation of what is expected from each team member.

Very needless to say, the plan is crucial to the success of the team because it provides the team with a strong sense of direction. This was very important in the situation I was in, for the team (prior to my arrival) had become disjointed and ultimately lost (i.e. without a clear or defined purpose) simply because they weren't operating from a plan.

This speaks to another critical aspect about a plan; that is the plan effectually unites the team. All it needs is a roadmap established upon the unification of each team member's several abilities and roles, a crucial factor which makes the plan both relevant and self-motivating for everyone involved.

Here's the clincher – the reason why the plan will always work is because it is an extension of the big apple. Accordingly, each team member is able to identify their unique path to their bite of the apple by simply understanding the plan.

In consequence, their initial hope and motivation will be translated into a great deal of confidence and trust because they can validate your vision for both corporate and personal success. You just have to get them to buy into your plan.

Fortunately I was able to get ample buy-in. As a matter of fact, this was the moment when things really began taking off for me and my team; for not only did I have a plan, I enlisted the team to help me finalize the plan.

Strategically this allowed me to ensure that the plan was a true reflection of everyone's reality (i.e. their strengths as well as their constraints). For this cause, my team dubbed me with the nickname "the man with the plan," a name which I cherish and thoroughly depicts how I live my life.

EXECUTING THE PLAN

What happened next is very simple. We executed the plan – and although I would love to tell you the plan worked to a tee, I would not violate the truth. See even though the plan was a good plan, it could not realistically account for the unknown. This is why the plan included auxiliary plans which described how we would handle the unexpected risks and issues which could not be accounted for at the outset of our merry little quest for projects success.

True to our profession, we referred to these auxiliary plans as back-up plans – and, as expected, these back-up plans saved us many times; for we were impacted by the unknown more times than even our most pessimistic team member had pre-calculated. Nevertheless, we were able to absorb these undesirable occasions and adjust as necessary for one simple reason – when things went south, we always had a back-up plan.

This speaks to another manner in which I live my life; that is without stress. How do I do this? The answer is simply by adequate planning, for planning is the key to preparedness and preparedness effectively eliminates stress.

Markedly this is a critical lesson for leaders. Reason being, if you are plagued by stress, chances are you will pass your stress on to your team members.

This is why I invest so much time in effective planning, for I am positioning myself to compromise my team's success if I allow myself to be victimized by stress. So take my advice, whether you are a leader or assigned to another role on the team, don't allow yourself to be afflicted by stress. Find a way to deal with it.

Do you like happy endings? I do and I have one for you. Due to an increasing measure of motivation and a well-crafted plan, we finished the next 3 projects successfully. As a result, what was once a series of dying project evolved into this corporation's most profitable program. All it took was a team of unique professionals modifying their perspectives on change and giving themselves to pursuing the opportunity of group success.

CHANGE AGENT

One of the greatest labels I've been given (and I've been given many) is a change agent. I'll never forget the day I walked into a co-worker's office and expressed my frustrations about the inefficiencies of a multi-million dollar project I was managing. My frustration – although the project was well-financed and backed up with thorough planning, the project team consistently failed in various areas of compliance. What is more, I could not convince the project stakeholders to enforce the rules which they ironically had put into place.

Now some might look at this scenario and consider this matter to be much to do about nothing. After all, this is how most of my co-workers and team members felt. Yet I was convinced these inefficiencies (over an extended period of time) would negatively impact the project because non-compliance is a patented slippery slope.

That's when I sought out a senior manager who I often turn to for professional guidance. Her advice to me then and on several other occasions was both direct and profound. Sagely she encouraged me to stand my ground; not necessarily because I was *right*, for predicting the future is hardly ever an exact science. On the contrary, she told me to stand up for my beliefs because I was *in the right*. There's a difference.

She also encouraged me to continue to stand tall even if I was standing alone. I, being both honest and whimsical, ensured her I would be (standing alone that is). She, being both wise and understanding, reminded me that I was a change agent and standing up for what's right is what change agents do. We know this because bringing about change almost always requires us to go against the social grain.

To make a long story short, my concerns were validated as the health of the project began to decline. What do you think the project stakeholders did then? You guessed it – they sent out high priority emails enforcing the compliance I had begged for many months in advance when things were going well.

In the end this project did finish on schedule. Yet we were over-budget; for even though we had corrected the project to the extent that the schedule was saved, the prior inefficiencies adversely skewed the finances. Subsequently, even though the project was in part successful, it was not nearly as successful as it could have been.

So what's the awesome moral of this story? After all, the project was not a complete success even though I stood my ground. Albeit this is true, critical lessons were learned and implemented on the ensuing project. Thus although we settled for less on the initial project, we positioned ourselves to succeed on the next one, and we did.

There I came to realize a critical reality; namely, we can recover from any mistake we make as long as we learn from it and avoid it the next time around – and trust me; there will be a "next time around."

Furthermore, because I had stood my ground and consistently voiced my concerns, I had increased my credibility in the eyes of the project stakeholders. As a result, they increased the efficiency of the ensuing project by enforcing additional standards which I convinced them would safeguard the project. So even though they chose to learn the hard way during the first project, they eventually realized 2 things: an ounce of prevention is worth a pound of cure, and do not ever underestimate the power of a change agent.

THE SUMMATION

As a result of the various seasons of change we must all endure in our lives, our destiny (although a singular path at the highest level) will surely cross over diverse terrains corresponding to the various life seasons. The principles I offer are structured to help you successfully navigate this path when it suddenly or gradually changes.

In this decisive order, you must first remember to always have a positive perspective. There's a reason why a prime facet of my personal brand is the thumbs-up sign. See it's a constant, oft personal reminder to always look on the bright side and to continually align my perspective with a reasonably worthy hope for the best.

It is also a consummate testament to the importance of balance as a focal aspect of progressive living. Consider this – in accordance to the law of averages, life is patently a "50-50" affair, for the sum of the challenges in your quest and the sum of the stretches highlighted by smoother sailing will even out in the long run.

Understanding this, your perspective is not an indicator of the quality of your life (seeing as everyone's life will be depicted by its fair share of crises). On the contrary, your perspective is a reflection of your personal fire to succeed each crisis and effectually save each cause. So make sure yours is always positive; less it becomes a deterrent to your fulfillment.

Upon employing a positive and applicable perspective, you must remain focused on your opportunities as they effectively light your path. Your opportunities are also collectively your primary source of motivation to succeed. So find them. Embrace them. Make the most of them.

To do so, you're going to have to formulate a plan. It doesn't need to be elaborate; neither do you need to be a professional planner to succeed. All you need is a set of goals and objectives which you can perform in sequence to cash in on your opportunities.

Then there's the unknown, a patented plan-crasher. No big deal; you own the unknown, for you are not limited to the upshot of Plan A. You wisely crafted a backup plan, a Plan B if you will. Consequently, if Plan A doesn't take you all the way, Plan B will; for when the unexpected happens and fate takes one of its twirling turns, you will use your backup plan and take the detour.

As a matter of fact, get used to taking the detour as it may very well account for nearly half of your journey. See there are many occasions in which we'll be forced to employ Plan B. For example, we will have to follow this order when we make crucial mistakes for a sure cause – mistakes always introduce new factors and new factors are a red flag for change.

We may also be forced to take the detour as a result of a mistake made by someone else. Do not be discouraged by this reality, for living a life of purpose is not about all the times we have to take a detour as a result of a mistake or any other mal-incident. No sir; living a life of purpose is about your burning desire to succeed every obstacle on your path and employing sound wisdom to ensure your quest is as uncomplicated as possible.

Last but not least, you can recover from any mistake as long as you are open to change. In line with this realism, I will offer a final word on change.

You can recover from any mistake as long as you learn from it and avoid it the next time around – and this is conclusive evidence proving you have changed.

CHAPTER 4

Fulfillment and Success

*

*"I searched for beauty as I climbed, an endless
mountain into time; I found fulfillment, ever
sublime; now I'm successful, now I am prime."*

LIFE'S GREATEST REWARD

Until now we have largely touched upon the concept of fulfillment and how it relates to the models of purpose and destiny. However, we have yet to address the related concept of success. Therefore, I would like to dedicate this lecture to analyzing the similarities and differences between fulfillment and success.

Right off the bat we can make a decisive conclusion concerning success; that is success is not on the same level as fulfillment with specific regards to the models of self-realization (i.e. understanding your purpose) and self-actualization (i.e. fulfilling your purpose).

Now before I move forward and elaborate on this statement, I will provide an applicable definition of fulfillment.

Fulfillment is the progressive realization of a purpose and/or the completion of an intrinsic need which can be applied to individual areas of our lives or universally.

Pragmatically fulfillment is the feeling you get once you achieve a focal aspect of your destiny. It is also, to lesser degrees, the experience of the actual pursuit.

Scientifically fulfillment is the coalescence of the experiences of self-realization and self-actualization. That is to say, you have not only established your life purposes. Courageously and with great wisdom, you have achieved each one in their currency.

A FEELING LIKE NO OTHER

Perceptibly the most attractive level of fulfillment is the plane of completion, simply because there's no higher level you can ascend to after you've reached the top.

I can speak to this matter from experience. When I was 20 years old I identified 1 of my life purposes. I was destined to write a thesis on scriptural theology utilizing a concept and a model very similar to the Pinnacle of Purpose which I designated as *"The Pinnacle of Holiness."* 9 years later I finally finished and published the book.

Now "on paper" one might consider this extended timeline and question whether or not this was truly 1 of my life purposes. Nonetheless, I assure each reader it was; specifically because the vast majority of those 9 years were not spent writing the book whatsoever. Rather they were semi-productive years marred by personal disillusionment, for I consistently allowed myself to be victimized by incessant distractions. Fatefully these prevented me from completing an assignment in the amount of time it should have originally taken (i.e. a little over 1 year).

Obviously I can recall the difficult path to completing this initiative. Yet even more so, I'll never forget the feeling of matchless fulfillment I experienced when the first copy came to me in the mail and I held it in my hands.

This relates back to my earlier assertion that fulfillment is greatest at the end of the journey, for both the journey and your levels of fulfillment are complete. Thus conclusively, it's the desire to achieve completeness which drives us to the finish line.

Then again, I'll never forget how one of my brothers just so happened to call me from Seattle at the time and encouraged me to take in the moment. It was such a profound and memorable experience that I literally sat there in an overwhelming yet tranquil state of euphoria for approximately 15 minutes.

Then at once I heard someone calling my name. So I looked around my loft, gazing across the room; but I could not detect anyone else around me. That's when I realized my brother was still on the phone. It was his voice I was hearing.

Clearly you don't have to be an author to relate to the feeling I had at that moment. I felt similar or greater feelings when I was married, became a father, graduated from college, and received major promotions. The point I'm trying to make is simply this – the feeling of fulfillment is like no other.

MODELS OF SUCCESS

I would at this time pivot our discussion to analyze success and how it relates to fulfillment. I would begin by stating a relative unknown – success both precedes and follows fulfillment. Ergo, success is a constant validation of our increasing levels of fulfillment.

Additionally our measures of success are dependent on our levels of fulfillment. Therefore, if you want to be successful in life, you must first seek after fulfillment. Else your pursuit of success alone will certainly leave you unfulfilled.

In proving this matter, and to further enhance our study, I will provide a definition of success with specific regards to the higher order of fulfillment.

Success is the purposeful completion of any milestone or objective on your path to fulfillment.

In line with this definition, our successful achievement of each milestone on our path to fulfillment brings us closer and closer to our destiny.

At the same time, success is also denoted by the attainment of wealth or other rewards due to the actions and volition of the one benefiting. Plainly speaking, our acquisition of success will be accompanied by various physical benefits (e.g. affluence or recognition).

Here lies the obvious glow of success, an immensely attractive glow which many of us are by and large driven by because it is highlighted by tangible rewards and the perceived great prospects of personal edification. See we are creatures of sight. Thus our leading motivations will generally be instigated by that which we can see.

Nevertheless, it is critical to understand that this tangible model of success is neither aligned nor equated to fulfillment. I can state this with certainty because fulfillment is a predominately intangible experience which can not be perfectly expressed with words. However, you know it when you have it because (as I said before) it is a feeling like no other.

THE EVOLUTION OF SUCCESS

This matter lends itself to the primary variance between fulfillment and the tangible model of success; namely fulfillment evolves internally while its focus is external. That is to say, your quest for fulfillment begins with you; yet it's not about you. Rather it's about all the people within your life offices (including you) and the righteous cause of corporate edification.

> *Seeing as no man is an island, we can not experience fulfillment apart from progressive interactions and involvements with others.*

On the other hand, the secondary (i.e. tangible) model of success not only evolves internally; its focus remains internal. Here lies a crucial problem which I will capture employing another interest point.

Notwithstanding, it is possible to achieve limited measures of success in this isolated manner; explicitly because the tangible model of success is patently individual-focused. This proves we can be successful on our own accord apart from the efforts of a larger whole.

Not only do many people realize this; a good portion have given themselves to pursuing this severely limited model of success. Unfortunately these do not realize how this avenue of success does not lead to fulfillment. The only model of success which does is the primary model which measures success by our completion of the objectives on our path to fulfillment.

This is universally evident, for this model of success does not exist apart from fulfillment – and although this model does yield physical benefits, these benefits are neither obtained nor pursued outside the over-arching model of fulfillment. Less they become greater than the cause of fulfillment and prevent you from fulfilling your purpose.

THE ICING AND THE CAKE

Utilizing my prior example concerning my purpose to publish a theological thesis, I would state the following – my success in this endeavor had nothing to do with how many books I would sell, how much money I would make, or the recognition I would receive for my efforts; for not only are these factors tangible, they are also unpredictable.

As such, they could not be attributed as prevailing factors of fulfillment seeing as fulfillment is delineated by a clear (i.e. predictable) path. Accordingly, the vast majority of my success in writing this thesis was contingent to the fact that I completed what was a major milestone on my path to fulfillment. This is the model of success which actually precedes fulfillment and thus serves as a primary validation.

I refer to this analysis as "the cake." The gist is all you really need is a cake to have dessert at a birthday party; albeit there will very likely be an assortment of sweets to go around.

A similar analysis would be likened to buying a car. Typically you don't buy a car for all the "bells and whistles." You buy a car for the purpose of resolving the specific need of getting you from Point A to Point B and preferably at an affordable price. Therefore, you're more interested in factors such as gas mileage and the overall quality of the car as opposed to auxiliary features such as the audio system or a moonroof.

This matter lends itself to all the tangible rewards which will follow our leading acquisition of success. These rewards constitute the icing on the cake, the bells and whistles on your car. They are "nice-to-haves," but they are not "must-haves."

This is precisely why they represent the secondary, lesser part of success. It is for this cause – you wouldn't buy a car primarily for the bells and whistles. You probably wouldn't secure the car you really need if you did. Thus you would likely find yourself wasting time and money in an endeavor which has meager prospects of fulfillment.

This is indeed why you must stay focused on purpose and first resolving those needs which provide fulfillment. Then you can look to adding the bells and whistles onto the vehicle you have already confirmed will get the job done. You can begin adding icing to your cake of choice.

In my case, I most certainly appreciate all the tangible rewards for my efforts in writing *"The Pinnacle of Holiness."* Yet they are not the primary reasons why I wrote the book. More than anything, I wrote the book to share knowledge on various theological topics.

This is exactly why I was so elated when I received the first copy, for my mission was complete. I had effectually made my cake. So I had a party, figuratively and literally.

From now, whatever happens with the book is the icing. This could be measured in book sales or in a whole host of ways which serve as added confirmation that publishing this book was truly my destiny and a worthwhile endeavor.

Still make no mistake about it. The greater part of my success has nothing to do with this future unknown, unquantifiable validation. Rather it has everything to do with the fact that I effectively fulfilled my purpose in publishing the book.

This brings me to my final word on this matter – there is very little use for icing without a cake. So take my advice and focus on obtaining success on your path to fulfillment, and don't be too concerned about the physical benefits succeeding. Neither set your heart on them; for in time they will come, in their own time, and every hour spent watching for them is an hour wasted.

THE PATH TO INDIVIDUAL SUCCESS

Here's another thing about the secondary model of success (which I will consciously refer to as *individual success* due to its self-centric focus). Those who follow after it alone will never find fulfillment simply because they are travelling the wrong way. This brings us to another interest point.

> **Just as there is a path to fulfillment, there also exists a path to individual success.**

Manifestly there are various stark differences between these 2 paths; explicitly the path to fulfillment leads all the way to the top of the Pinnacle of Purpose while its counterpart doesn't. As a matter of fact, the path to individual success is a cul-de-sac which concludes with an impenetrable impasse. Tis a far cry from the path to fulfillment, a path which progressively leads us into new seasons and advanced stages of our destiny.

Now this is only 1 manner in which these 2 paths are dissimilar. Here's another – unlike the path of fulfillment, which is unrelenting and provides compounded measures of contentment, the path to individual success is often lonely and persistently wearisome.

For this cause, many who singly follow after success will not only come to a dead-end in their pursuit; they will eventually wear themselves out and become stuck. Like a car out of gas, they will be parked stationary on the edge of the highway of life while others are passing them by.

As bleak as this reality is (and it is), there is a ray of hope. The key lies in a principle we spoke to in the prior lecture; that is every progressive path in our life ultimately leads to our destiny. Therefore, as the pursuit of individual success is not without purpose, it is possible to merge onto the path to

fulfillment from this constricted path. So even if we are not perfectly on the optimal path of life, our destiny is still in play as long as we have purpose.

FULFILLMENT PROVIDES ENDURING SUCCESS

Now the summation of this lecture is a principle I've come to refer to as the *"Destiny Principle."* It reveals the following:

Success is always a part of fulfillment and can only be experienced in full on the path to fulfillment. In every other model, we would be relegated to only achieving success in part and fail to fulfill our purpose.

This principle validates my earlier assertion that our focus in life should be on obtaining fulfillment as opposed to success. Otherwise our measures of success will be curtailed and we will remain unfulfilled.

You don't have to take my word for it. Just look around and you will find that some of the most successful people in life (by society's standards) are simultaneously some of the least fulfilled.

From where I stand this is no paradox. On the contrary, and in line with all the principles we have discussed thus far, it is to be expected. Therefore, as you follow your path to fulfillment, ascending your unique pinnacle of purpose, do not allow yourself to become distracted with success factors which are not perfectly aligned with your destiny.

True, this will not be a simple matter, for these success factors provide various benefits (e.g. feelings of security, greater opportunities for wealth, and other manners of physical increase). The problem is none of these benefits will last forever.

Furthermore, they will always be reduced to vanity simply because you are yet unfulfilled. Conclusively, in spite of all these success factors, you will retain a certain emptiness and a longing to be complete.

At last, this is why we all must find fulfillment; for only fulfillment provides us with enduring success, and there is an inherent desire within all of us to be successful.

THE SUMMATION

Everyone desires to experience fulfillment and success. The problem is too many of us go about our search in a less-than-effective manner. As a result, we only experience success in part and retain our longing to be fulfilled.

Nevertheless, if we commit ourselves to the path of fulfillment, we will incur all the success this life can afford us. This brings me to my final word on this lecture.

A successful man who is unfulfilled is a lonely man who will eventually find himself going nowhere. Therefore, strive to be fulfilled and do not let success within and of itself distract you from relentlessly seeking after your purpose.

CHAPTER 5

The Transition to Purpose

*

"I found myself without a cause, without a purpose,
without a law; Then I considered all my flaws,
and worked to change what I'd become."

DO YOUR BEST

Unlike some kids I really enjoyed school. However, I enjoyed school much more prior to the 8th grade. Here's the reason why – I entered a new school system that year which was not nearly as advanced as the one I had come out of. Accordingly, academic success required a greater investment and commitment to excellence on my part prior to 8th grade.

As for me, I do my best work when I am either challenged or under pressure. Like a small fraction of our world population, I love the big stage. I live for the moment when the stakes are highest and I can't remember the last time I shied away from a challenge. Whether it was education, sports, or games in general, I was always going to give 110% because I wanted to win more than anything.

Now that was when I was a very young man and didn't realize there was more to life than winning. Then one day it hit me. We had just lost the championship game in a basketball tournament by 2 points. Then came the agonizing scene of watching the winning team as they celebrated, followed by the somber ride home.

To make this loss even harder to swallow, I had undeniably played the best organized game of my entire life. Still it wasn't enough for us to win the game – and as the captain of the team I felt particularly responsible; like I had let the team down.

So there I was, on the doorstep of the throes of defeat when it hit me – I had done my best even though we lost the game. Not just me, but the entire team played their hearts out to win. We just happened to play a better team on that day.

Moreover, we were missing one of our best players; our starting point guard to be precise. Yet in spite of that fact, we put forth a valiant effort and almost pulled off the upset; crucial facts I was only able to consider and appreciate after I had begun the oft difficult search for the proverbial silver lining.

It was exactly then that I realized you can experience both fulfillment and success without winning. From this truth follows the well-known cliché "winning isn't everything." We know this because the same way you can find fulfillment while sustaining a loss, you can obtain a victory and simultaneously be unfulfilled.

Once I realized this, I stopped focusing so much on winning and shifted my motivation to the source of the fulfillment I experienced after losing the championship game; namely the fact that I had given my best effort.

There I realized that winning the game was not my truest desire; not at all. My truest desire was doing my best to win the game. Trust me; there's a huge difference.

In realizing this, I felt the immense weight associated with the fear of losing fall off my shoulders; for as I had come to know the true meaning of fulfillment, I had redefined the standards of winning and losing. Here's what I came up with – the only way to lose in life is by failing to do your best. For that reason, the most authentic spectrum of winning is broader than society (specifically sports) often portrays it.

This speaks to why I don't over-concern myself with winning and losing by society's standards, for these models are based upon factors beyond my control. Instead I concern myself with one of the few things I can control; that is the amount of effort I'm going to put forth to be successful in every endeavor.

Here is the conclusion of this matter – if you can channel your energies toward doing your best as opposed to just merely winning, you will understand the difference between fulfillment and success (win or lose) while having the great pleasure of experiencing both.

EVERYTHING I WANTED

I can't tell you how much I wish I realized this in those days, for I would not have failed to consistently do my best early on in life if I had. Yet seeing as I did fail on this wise, I regrettably left a great deal of fulfillment on the table.

This speaks to why I enjoyed school so much prior to 8th grade. It is because I was consistently challenged, a challenge being one of the few motivating factors which prompted me to consistently perform. Inorganic as it was (and it was), it routinely brought out the best in me.

Unfortunately I never consistently felt this challenge in high school, and so I under-achieved. Then life took one of its fateful turns and I came face to face with the greatest challenges of my life up until that point in time – college.

Needless to say, graduating from college was one of the major milestones on my path to fulfillment and a certain high-stakes proposition. Therefore I, true to form and perceiving the immense challenge of graduating from college, was highly motivated to succeed.

3 years later I successfully declared, "Mission complete." I had finished my undergraduate career with a B.S. in Computer Science/Management Information Systems at the ripe age of 20. The only thing standing between me and my post-graduate life was a year-long internship with a software firm in Carmel, IN.

Truly those were some pretty intense days. I had a schedule overload nearly every semester, I attended every summer school session, I had a part-time job the entire time, I faithfully attended church services throughout the week and on the weekends; the list goes on.

Now I'm not stating any of this to boast, for none of this is worthy of boasting. I do however want to make a point with regards to my levels of dedication to the goal. Graduating from college was one of my life purposes – and although I wasn't prepared for it in the beginning (for we are hardly ever truly prepared for anything in life), I took it seriously. I stayed focused. I made it happen.

Advantageously I carried this momentum into the next phase of my life. At 21 I started my professional career as a software developer. By the time I was 25, I had become an IT director managing a group of senior consultants, program managers, and project managers – and by the time I was 28, I had started my own small business which I ran while continuing to work as a consultant in the IT field. A year later I became a published author.

In my own eyes I was building a semi-impressive resume fairly quickly. By the time I was 30, I had spent over half my professional career as a senior-level manager and was making more money than I had planned when I began my career only 10 years earlier. I had my own family, a brand new home which we built and custom designed, and many other tangible rewards. Ultimately I had everything I wanted in life – or so I thought.

MY INFLEXION POINT

The truth is that even though I had accomplished so much and reaped a great deal of fruit from my labor, I was not happy; for although I had become completely unaware of it, I had desires (i.e. life purposes) which were not being fulfilled. Consequently, those 10 years of terrific individual success were marred by difficult personal times and an increasing sense that I was living outside of my true purpose. Still the focal question I would like to address is – why wasn't I happy?

You should know the answer by now. Quite simply, I was unhappy because I was unfulfilled. This matter lends itself to an assessment I made in the previous lecture; expressly, only fulfillment provides complete and enduring success. Therefore, as my success was predominately obtained outside of my path to fulfillment, it was neither complete nor enduring. Almost 10 years into my professional career, the light bulb finally stopped flickering. Then suddenly it went off.

So what did I do? Well first of all, I did a rewind on my life so that I could rediscover and reconsider my truest desires. It was exactly then that I realized that being a senior manager in IT was never my "dream." My dream (i.e. primary life purpose) was to be a teacher so that I could utilize my greatest gift (i.e. writing) and my greatest passion (i.e. education).

I am pretty sure I know the question most readers are asking at this point, so I will ask it on your collective behalf – if I knew this all along (i.e.

that I was destined to be a teacher and a writer), how did I stumble into IT and why have I been in IT for over 15 years?

The answer is as classic as it is sure – my dad had convinced me to go to college for computer science primarily because he was not interested in paying for me to go to college to become a teacher or a writer. Fair enough; I was pretty adept with computers and was a pretty decent coder in high school, so it made sense to me.

Furthermore, those were the late 1990's and information technology was on the rise to say the least. So getting a good-paying job right after college and becoming self-sufficient was not going to be an issue (a crucial matter because my dad had also let me know that my permanent residency at Hotel Anderson expired after I turned 18).

Then again, I (poor man that I was) admittedly was not interested in paying for my tuition. So I willingly signed on the dotted line. I was getting a B.S. in Computer Science/Management Information Systems.

Now even though I made this concession, I promised myself that I would eventually do all those things which brought me fulfillment – and I wasn't going to wait until I was 80 years old to do so. No, I was going to make the transition as soon as I could; specifically once I was in a good financial state. So even though I was taking a brief detour from my original path to fulfillment, I felt like I had a pretty good plan to get back on my destiny track.

GETTING BACK ON TRACK

The problem is I didn't stick to the plan; for as I became increasingly successful in my IT career, I began to invest increasingly more time in my professional office. Here lies the inflexion and what became an immense problem. Explicitly, I became so enthralled with the increasing success of my IT career that it became a distraction; to the point where I had gotten side-tracked with regards to my quest for fulfillment.

This is a classic example of the variance between individual success and fulfillment. I can state this with certainty because of the primary reason why I increased my investment in my career; that would be the tangible rewards. Alas, over time I became so highly driven by these rewards that I lost sight of my original plans to become a professional writer and educator.

To make matters worse, I never thoughtfully considered the impact this distraction was having on those around me. Therefore, understanding how my pursuit of individual success had distracted me for several years, I purposefully used it as a launching pad for my personal quest for fulfillment.

Traditionally this is one of my favorite strategies in life. Many refer to it as "making the best of a not-so-great situation." I love it because it allows us to get the most out of every situation, which is crucial because inevitably not every enterprise will be 100% efficient.

This goes back to 2 assertions I've made in prior chapters. Firstly, we can recover from any miscalculation we make in life as long as we are willing to invest more energy and effort in recovery than we did in descending into any unfulfilling state – and secondly, it is possible to merge onto the path to fulfillment from the path to individual success. I know because that's exactly what I did once I realized these 2 paths were not the same, and that I had not made the most out of my professional or social career in spite of all my success.

It was at that time that I sensed another challenge; perhaps the greatest challenge of my entire life. I was going to have to find a way to get back onto my path to fulfillment after years of traveling in the wrong direction.

This may not sound like a huge deal on paper; yet trust me, it's a very complex situation for the following cause — life happens in real-time. You don't get a do-over if you mess up and there are no off-setting penalties which allow you to "replay the down."

What is more, thousands of events related to your destiny have already been set in motion. Accordingly, and with great wisdom and precision, you will have to account for them all in order to get back on track.

In my case, I was already in multiple professional and social offices. Consequently, getting back onto my path to fulfillment was not something I could just do overnight. Conversely, it would require a great deal of prudence, planning, and patience, for it was incumbent upon me to ensure this transition was as smooth as possible. Less I allow another miscalculation on my part to adversely impact those within my life offices.

Figuratively it's like in the movies when you have the hero trying to jump from one road vehicle to another while both are traveling at awesome speeds. Here's the difference — unlike the star-studded actor in the big screen, you don't have a stunt double taking on the most difficult assignments. No sir; the hero trying to make this impossible, death-defying leap in this high-stakes action scene is you.

This is precisely why getting back on track is no small matter, for life happens at a similarly accelerating speed which is as constant as it is real. So take my advice and don't rush the transition from your current path to your destined path. Instead allow it to happen naturally, for nature has a way of working things out in your favor so long as you have purpose.

As for me, I was all about purpose; not just because I was intent on achieving complete levels of fulfillment, but because I was also determined to capitalize on my distractions and delays to make up for lost time. See I find any form of waste to be persistently vexing. Therefore, this was one matter I was fully prepared to see through. I was not only all-in. I was going for broke.

MY LIFE PINNACLES STORY

That's when I began to formulate the basis for Life Pinnacles, a program which would not only allow me to find fulfillment in my life; it would be structured in such a universal way that it would do the same for others who applied the same principles in their lives. It is the climax of my destiny and that which the world will remember me best by after the days of my life are fulfilled.

So how did Life Pinnacles allow me to find fulfillment in my life? The answer is sure – Life Pinnacles allows me to spend every hour of my day doing those things which I was designed to do, wherein lies my fulfillment.

Not only this, but the various messages I speak to in this program lay out both universal and comprehensive paths which allowed me to ascend to this model way of life. This is why I am convinced the program is destined to be successful, for its universal nature qualifies everyone in our world for fulfillment while its comprehensive qualities make each singular path easy to understand.

It begins with discovering your life purposes, internal desires wholly reflective of your unique individual being. From there you must look to join various professional and social offices through which you can fulfill these purposes (e.g. a family of your own, a professional office to utilize your strengths, or a non-profit organization to support your community).

Then, understanding the demands of each office, you must commit yourself to daily giving your best effort towards the fulfillment and success of each office. It's a grind, I know, but one which you will appreciate immensely simply because you are living a life of purpose. Thus for every bead of sweat you perspire executing your life's work, you will acquire new energies significantly greater than those which you originally exerted. These will replenish you and position you to keep each of your offices moving forward.

Lastly you must devote yourself to living a progressive spiritual life, following all the "golden rules," and working towards ensuring all your interactions with your fellow man reflect the superlative nature of our Creator.

At a 10,000 foot elevation, this is the basis of the Life Pinnacles program. It is a series of progressive messages which take on the forms of pinnacles, roadmaps, and timelines, and effectively lead men and women towards their destiny. All the while, they are steadily increasing their levels of fulfillment and success.

In my case, Life Pinnacles has allowed me to reach a point in my life where I am able to both write and educate (i.e. my 2 primary life purposes) without any undue pressure or stress. Money is not an issue. Time is not an issue. The truth is there are no issues, a testimony to the simplistic nature of the path to fulfillment.

All the same, it is important to note that I didn't get here overnight; not even close. If you were under this impression, I call you to remember my earlier analysis which spoke to how life happens in real-time (an analysis which spoke to the difficulty of merging onto the path of fulfillment after spending an extended period of time on another path).

Allow me to be frank – raising a family in the 21st century isn't cheap. I would argue that it's more expensive than it has ever been and requires a greater investment of each parent's time to ensure each child is wholly positioned to achieve fulfillment and success in their own lives.

So was money an issue in getting back onto my destiny track? You bet money was an issue. Similarly was time an issue? You bet time was an issue. The question is – how did I address it?

Well fortunately my pursuit of individual success was not without reward. Hence I was able to obtain enough wealth to initiate my Life Pinnacles program straightaway. Yet I didn't have the wealth to grow the program apart from my professional career.

This matter lends itself to the associative time and suitability factors with regards to my professional career. Unlike some individuals who are not as fortunate as I am, I thoroughly enjoy my work. Truly the field of information technology has been very good to me; primarily because of all the intangible benefits and, to lesser degrees, the tangible rewards.

As for the tangible rewards, we've already discussed how these helped me get back on my destiny track. As for the intangible benefits, these constitute a whole array of openings and occasions which are wholly aligned with my gift of writing and my passion for education – and although I didn't consider it before, I eventually came to the realization that my professional career had given me ample opportunities to increase both my writing and education skills.

Furthermore, I was also given opportunities to increase my leadership, presentation, and a plethora of other skills which have in effect made me more effective in all my other offices. Most importantly, they helped mold me into a man capable of managing all the business aspects associated with launching any operational program.

This brings me to the time factor. In times past I regularly pushed to work as many hours as it took to get the job done, which on some occasions meant working upwards to 80 hours in 1 week.

Presently I don't push as hard; neither will I enter into a position where excessive hours are the norm. Less I am forced to make concessions in the evolution of my other offices.

Now I do concede that I have been forced to relinquish certain avenues of success in the process – and that's ok. With all my present commitments to my current life offices, the time just isn't there.

What is there is a clear path before me which I can testify from experience is increasingly fulfilling. Hereafter (and as my grandmother would say), I'm going to walk on this road until my feet get bare.

At a high level, this is *"My Life Pinnacles Story."* It's the story about a young man who knew what he wanted out of life but got side-tracked for reasons which at this point don't matter. It's the narrative of a plucky, yet unlikely hero who devoted himself to every cause required to align himself with his destiny; who somehow, someway found the path and stuck with it until it brought him to the place where he was originally destined to be.

Your story may be quite different than mine. Still I promise you the end result will be the same – a fulfilling life of purpose which grows sweeter as the days go by.

Likewise it doesn't matter if your transition onto your path to fulfillment is not as straightforward as another's. In fact, it may be downright complicated. Most transitions of this magnitude are. Nevertheless, if you follow the path I lay out in this series of lectures and compositions, you will find success, fulfillment, and ultimately your destiny while authoring your very own "My Life Pinnacles Story."

BUT NOW

Before moving on to discuss the 7 levels of the Pinnacle of Purpose, I want to share 2 of the most important words of all time – *but now.* Besides being 2 words almost always used at the beginning of a sentence, "but now" corresponds to some of the greatest, most critical moments in life. This is yet another matter I can testify to from experience.

"Everyone needs a *but now* moment," I avowed to a group of young people at a forum. I had been asked to speak to them concerning what it means to live a life of purpose and what fulfilling your destiny looks like.

Now perceiving how few to none understood where I was going with this declaration, I continued by professing, "But now represents the moment in your life when you turn the corner with regards to any purposeful initiative. It's the moment when everyone and everything which was against you becomes silent because you were right about your destiny and they were wrong – and because you valiantly endured all things to win the prize, you have now transcended purpose and crossed the lofty plane of fulfillment. You, my friend, have overcome."

To this day I remember the room becoming so silent that you could hear the clock on the wall ticking; it was that quiet. I surmise it's because the young people in the audience were really hearing what I had to say. Due to some unique event in their individual lives, they knew exactly where I was coming from and could perceive where I was going with this line of discussion. So I continued.

"But now is an experience highlighted by a calm enduring moment when you encounter an internal peace; where you consider all the things you have borne. You consider the pain, the mistakes, the sorrow, the shame, and what do you do? Do you wallow in sadness? Are you buried beneath the persistent flood of missed opportunities or the intense pangs of regret and fear?"

I paused after asking these questions to add emphasis to my inquiry, but more so to take survey of my audience. Then, for the first time during that lecture, I felt like everyone present was literally on the edge of their seat. That's when I partly smiled as I shook my head. Then I answered my inquiry replying, "No, you don't; not you, for your mind is fixed on that which is imminent. Your eyes are set on the amazing opportunity of redemption as you perceive this truth – the future is untouched and your destiny will forever and always be within your hands. As long as you have breath, it will always be within your grasp.

All you have to do is reach out and take a hold of it. With great resolve and authority, reclaim what is yours. Reclaim what may have been lost, but what in the end is going to save you. Reclaim what is going to bring back your being and make you whole again."

I then looked at the audience one final time and simply reminded them of this moment saying, "But now…" Then at once I concluded my presentation, returned to my place on the stage and took my seat.

Now I don't measure the quality of my delivery by the response I get from the audience. However, I'm not sure I received a more spirited applause than I did that afternoon. Here's why – everyone in the world, whether they realize it or not, is in pursuit of their own "but now moment." The problem is many of us don't know what it looks like; neither do we know how to get there.

Nevertheless, by the conclusion of that particular presentation, everyone in the audience came to know both – and I conjecture many of them began making plans that very night to initiate their own search.

THE GREATEST HOPE FOR TOMORROW

It goes without saying that the hope of experiencing this critical moment helped carry me along my path to fulfillment. I mean no one works this hard at any initiative without expecting to be compensated in some manner.

Fortunately for us purpose seekers, this is one of the few endeavors in life where the reward is infinitely greater than the investment. Hence we stay.

Moreover, the opportunity to transcend all of my opposition and the realization of continued peace were more than enough to keep me on the path. Now if you've never been hated on or experienced a sleepless night, then you may not understand where I'm coming from. See life is not perfect where I come from; neither is it fair – and as fate would have it, most of the people I've come to know live under like circumstances. Therefore, it is highly unlikely that any of us are going to travel through life carefree or without a righteous desire for personal validation.

So as you read through the remaining chapters in this composition, do not be discouraged about where you are at in life or where you have been; neither be discouraged by any of the occasions which lack edification. Rather be encouraged about where you are going. Be invigorated by who you will become at the end of your journey and the process of transformation which transpires in between, for it represents the greatest hope for tomorrow.

Furthermore, don't be distracted by all the haters, doubters, and all the other tragic characters of life. Neither be disheartened by all the troubles you will have to endure to achieve fulfillment, for all which you refuse to allow to break you will only make you stronger – and all these things work together to increase the significance and the power of your "but now moment."

PREVAILING PRINCIPLES

Now before I conclude this chapter, I would like to recap the 3 primary principles we have discussed thus far. These principles should be kept in mind as we go through the remaining chapters unveiling the 7 levels of the Pinnacle of Purpose.

1. **The Change Principle:** Referred to as the *"Great Human Dilemma,"* change is the baseline of your quest for fulfillment and ultimately your destiny. This is evident by the multiple variations of your life purposes. So do not resist progressive change, for in each instance change represents the exit ramp which takes you from one season in your life to the next.

2. **The Treasure Principle:** Your heart is the location of your treasures in life. Therefore, to make the most of the opportunities presented to you, you must first comprehend the immense value of each opportunity life presents you with and come to see them as distinct treasures. Only then will your heart truly be involved.

3. **The Destiny Principle:** Success can not be fully realized apart from fulfillment. Therefore, your focus should be on being fulfilled (as opposed to being successful) as this will allow you to eventually acquire the fullest measures of both of these noteworthy experiences.

THE SUMMATION

Upon understanding the nature of the path to fulfillment, many of us are going to make a crucial discovery; that is we are not on this pivotal path. No matter, for I will provide explicit instructions and guidelines to assist each reader in migrating onto this path regardless of what path you are presently on.

Notwithstanding, making this transition will not be a simple enterprise. It will be filled with various challenges, difficulties, mistakes, regrets, and the like. However, we can not allow for any of these to discourage us or prevent us from reaching our ultimate goal. Instead we must be consistently propelled by the ever-present opportunities of recovery and transcendence, and the realization of 2 simple words – but now. This brings me to my final word on the transition to living a life of purpose.

> **Everyone wants to be fulfilled in life. However, to have the fulfillment we seek, we must first understand what it takes to merge onto the singular path which affords it. Then we must endure all things to walk the path and ultimately reach its conclusion.**

CHAPTER 6

Confidence

*

"There are many things I can't conceive; I'll never know, I'll never perceive; Though this is true, why should I grieve? For in myself I do believe."

WE ALL BELIEVE IN YOU

Now that we have discussed the fundamentals of living a life of purpose, I would like to spend the remaining lectures in this composition speaking to the 7 levels of the Pinnacle of Purpose. I will begin by dedicating this chapter to critiquing confidence.

It should come as no surprise to any that confidence is the first level of the Pinnacle of Purpose. Conclusively, if you're going to fulfill your life purposes, you must first have confidence in yourself and your ability to achieve each one. Otherwise your lack of faith in yourself will cause you to stumble at some point on your path.

I would at this time put forth a question to each of my readers – when teaching this lesson to others, what do you think is the most common response I get at this point? Amazingly I almost always have at least one person suggest they are (for some unknown and often unfounded reason) not good enough to warrant their own endorsement – and although it's sometimes hard for me to get them to admit it, they usually have these sentiments because they're comparing themselves to someone else.

Here lies the problem. Comparing yourself to someone else is one of the most devastating actions you could ever take because your assessment will never be accurate. Neither will it ever be productive. What is certain is this – every time you compare yourself to someone else, you both increase the inefficiency of your perspective and decrease your self-worth.

Now the obvious question is – why even go there? It's hard enough trying to employ a positive perspective in every life situation. Why compound such a delicate matter with a non-value activity such as making a comparison?

Allow me to give you my advice. Not only is comparing yourself against others in isolation unwise; it is even less productive for this cause – no one can fulfill your life offices better than you. Ergo, it's not a matter of comparing yourself to others. When it comes to your destiny, no one compares to you! You are the standard, and all the gifts and talents you have both inherited and acquired will empower you to manifest your greatness to the world. The first thing you have to do is believe in yourself.

For those who feel better about having the support of others, I "feel you." Really, I do understand; specifically because I've been there and I've felt that way too. Therefore, if you are willing to increase your levels of self-confidence, I promise you will not be alone. In spirit I'll be right there with you, and so will countless others who are on a similar path. So you are not alone. We all believe in you.

THE OVERCONFIDENT WILL UNDERACHIEVE

As for me, I didn't have too much trouble with confidence; at least not at the beginning. I spent most of my youth in gifted and talented programs, had the opportunity to skip 2 grades, and was often regarded as one of the smartest persons in my classes. Inopportunely these factors caused me to (at times) become overconfident to my hurt.

The most prominent hurt was a sharp decline in my level of motivation, for I consciously curtailed my efforts whenever school became effortless. Sadly I only worked hard enough to get good-enough grades instead of the grades I was capable of, and was scarcely motivated to do my best if there was no challenge or high reward involved.

This example speaks to a very important lesson I have learned in life; namely, we can not fulfill our life purposes apart from excellence. Visibly this is a critical lesson, which is why excellence represents another life pinnacle; in particular, the life pinnacle which succeeds purpose.

Here's how excellence relates to confidence – excellence is the greatest source of any confidence we should have in ourselves; for we are fatally overconfident in any other scenario, and wholly situated for a fall.

My wake-up call came during my first semester in college. As fate would have it, the Computer Science program at Ball State University combined graduate and undergraduate courses. As a result, most of my computer science courses included graduate students who would routinely skew the grading curve.

Consequently, because my inclination towards overconfidence caused me to develop a fatal predisposition to settle for less than my best in high school, I spent almost 2 semesters in college adapting to the model of excellence and becoming academically competitive; specifically in those courses which were being dominated by grad students.

Still it took a considerable amount of time and energy to ascend to this level. Moreover, I had regrettably underachieved for 2 semesters. Thus I came to learn a crucial life lesson – the overconfident are some of the most patented underachievers in life.

NEVER CONCEDE THE HIGH GROUND

All things considered, I have met more persons lacking confidence than those who are overconfident. This is because our confidence usually diminishes as we grow older and apart from our destiny. This model is then negatively compounded by various tragic characters we'll be introduced to on our quest for fulfillment (e.g. haters, doubters, and liars).

Now it would be imprudent for me to address such a sad cast of characters individually. Thus I would do so collectively by making a leading assessment – most of the haters, doubters, and liars in your life are jealous of you. The question is *why?*

Like most questions, there are various answers to this most common inquiry. I'll address 2 leading with the following assessment – these individuals are comparing themselves to you, an action which we have already determined is as unproductive as it is unwise. Yet in doing so, they become disheartened because their reality is (by their inaccurate standards) not as good as yours.

Here lies the shady inflexion; for instead of working towards improving their reality, they would rather invest time and energy discrediting yours. These actions are taken primarily because they aren't going anywhere in life due to unwise decisions they've made and continue to make. Besides this, it takes far less effort to attack someone else's character than to build your own.

As for you, your decisions in life are the reason why you're going places. Furthermore, your decision not to stoop down to the level of those losing in life will insulate you against any natural fallout. I can state this with certainty due to a crucial life lesson which I will offer as an interest point.

> **In the end and after all, you will surely reap what you sow.**

Trust me; if I know anything I do know this — what goes around eventually comes around. Call it karma or the divine yet often inexplicable designs of cause and effect. We will all eventually get what's coming to us one way or the other.

Therefore, as we clearly perceive throwing stones is both a poor venture and a bad investment, we will surely encounter various losses and setbacks if we take this path.

You must believe me; it will never be worth it, for those losing in life are already miserable. What more of an effect could your throwing stones have on them?

Then again, the effect you may be looking for is not going to be the one you get for the following cause — it's practically impossible to get even in any life matter involving feelings and emotions. Your success rate will be less than 0.01%.

So if you're being hated on, do not allow yourself to be deceived into trying to get even. It's not going to happen. What will happen is this — the stone you throw trying to repay the favor is going to come back and hurt you even more than you intended to hurt the individual you threw it at.

My recommendation then is simple. Seeing how we are unable to get even in every life matter and life is consistently unfair, strive to be the bigger person in every situation and always stay on the high ground.

THE PATH WHICH LEADS NOWHERE

The second reason why some are jealous of you is because they have regrettably lost any sense of purpose in their own life. The reason for this letdown is inconsequential. The results will always be devastating, for these individuals will become fatally focused on being someone they're not and will never be. Consequently, they will invest a great deal of energy in various endeavors and on diverse paths which all lead nowhere.

No doubt this is a depressing model. It is also one I have a great deal of sympathy for; specifically because it is extremely distressing to constantly arrive at seemingly endless dead-ends in life.

See I know from experience, for I've suffered the immense distress which comes with being lost and continually arriving at dead-ends in various turns. I would at this time share one such occasion.

Now I wouldn't call myself a city-boy per se. Yet I was born and raised in suburban America and have spent a good deal of time in the city. So I'm used to seeing street signs, offices, grocery stores, and gas stations on every other block.

As for my wife, she was born and raised in the country. There the street signs are few and far in between – and unlike the comforts of my suburban stomping grounds, the street signs don't have names like White River Road, Main Street, or Fifth Avenue. They have numbers and a single letter like 100 W and 200 S (I later realized what these stood for).

One fateful afternoon I was going to visit my wife before we were married. I'd been to her house a time or 2 and was confident I would get there and return straightaway. Boy was I wrong! What should have been a 60-minute trip took almost 3 hours.

Mind you these were the days when GPS was new and not every car had a gizmo which told you what direction you were driving in. Even though some did, I was in college at the time. Thus to say I was a poor man would be a severe understatement. I was beyond poor. I was flat-out broke and the car I was driving at the time had no such luxury.

What I remember about that disastrous adventure was the feeling I kept getting whenever I hit a dead-end or came to the realization that I was on a road too long to be going in the right direction. Trust me; it's a terrible feeling, the feeling you are getting nowhere fast although you desperately want to be somewhere and are investing a great deal of energy trying to get there. In the most intense cases it can even bring you to tears.

Unfortunately this is how many who are losing in life feel every day. They are constantly spinning their wheels while the rest of the world is moving ahead.

True, this doesn't justify their malicious actions. Yet it explains them while providing us with a clear warning; namely, if you don't have confidence in yourself and your ability to fulfill every purpose associated with your destiny, you will become lost among the highways of life and consequently disillusioned.

What is worse, you will eventually become someone you never thought you'd be for one reason – you're heading down a path which leads nowhere; unambiguously nowhere close to true you.

TURNING THROWING STONES INTO STEPPING STONES

All these things lead us to a critical question – how should we deal with the haters and doubters in our lives?

Now in a previous section I said I would show you how to turn throwing stones into stepping stones to help you get where you want to be in life. At this time I would like to discuss how this happens starting with an example from my own life.

I was a freshman at Ball State University and barely a few days into my college career when I met with my guidance counselor for the first time. I knocked on the door to his office and peeked inside because the door was open. Then he looked up at me and asked who I was and what I wanted. So I introduced myself and told him we had a meeting scheduled. He quickly looked over his schedule and then finally invited me into his office.

Undesirably he was aloof the entire time I was there. Amidst all my questions and concerns, he decided it was more important to check his email and attend to other matters as opposed to giving me his undivided attention.

Still that didn't bother me so much. What did bother me was his response after I asked him what kind of job I could expect to land after I graduated. To this day I'll never forget how he looked at me with intense skepticism and said, "You'll probably be typing papers for your boss."

Now some would have expected me to get upset about this man's unwarranted condescension towards me. After all, he was my guidance counselor. He should have been supportive and encouraging; specifically because he didn't "know me from Adam." What reason did he have for making such a demeaning statement about someone he didn't even know?

Let's call it what it is. Whether he was miserable with his own life, prejudiced, or just having a bad day, he was essentially throwing a stone at me without a just cause.

Nevertheless, his disparagement towards me wasn't the most important thing; neither are all the haters and doubters in your life. What is important is how you are going to respond; that is the same way I responded to my unhelpful guidance counselor. You turn their negativity into positive energy by converting their derogatory remarks into a progressive challenge. Then you protect yourself from dwelling on their hatred and doubting by focusing on achieving whatever they said you couldn't do; so long as these accusations are in line with your purpose (which they often are).

This is precisely how their throwing stone becomes your stepping stone. When you effectively turn their disparaging comments into a progressive challenge, they acquire the ability to lift you up as opposed to tear you down. The only question is – are you up for the challenge?

THE ART OF FIGHTING WITHOUT FIGHTING

As for me, I was more than up for the challenge. As I said before, I live for a challenge and the opportunity to enter the big stage. It's where I do my best work; even in situations marked by conflict.

At the same time, being willing to address conflict didn't necessarily mean I would be successful at handling it. Truthfully I didn't become regularly successful in my management of conflict until I understood how every conflict retains a unique opportunity for good. Subsequently, it is possible (sometimes likely) for all parties to be edified by succeeding conflict. All it takes is one person who can see above the stress factors associated with someone throwing stones at them and effectively convert these stress factors into positive energy.

I refer to this example as "the art of fighting without fighting," a very popular model in the worlds of martial arts and medicine. At a very high level, this discipline encourages its followers to seek resolution without force under the crucial premise of *primum non nocere*. That is to say, first do no harm.

Now this model plays itself out in many ways. In the film "Enter the Dragon," martial arts master Bruce Lee portrays this superior fighting style when challenged by a visibly irritable man, a bully of sorts as witnessed by his disturbing desire to intimidate others. Thus to no one's surprise, this man wanted to take Bruce Lee on.

Big mistake! Many in the martial arts world consider Bruce Lee to be the greatest master of all time. Consequently, our villain here was undoubtedly preparing to get his hat handed to him.

This is when Bruce Lee moved to show the power of his preferred fighting style. See although he could have put the beat-down on this sad scoundrel, he wanted to make a crucial point about the most superior fighting style which I will reveal as an interest point.

> Your greatest show of strength is not in using your power in retaliation. On the contrary, your greatest show of strength is your refusal to fight back; particularly when you have the greater power to do so.

Now here's what happened next – Bruce Lee convinced the man to fight him on an island. Yet when the bully got in the boat to go toward the island, Bruce Lee didn't follow. Rather he let the boat get away from the ship with the bully in it all by himself. There he was, all alone in this small boat some 50 feet away from the ship with Bruce Lee holding the connecting line.

All things considered, this example speaks to delayed or evolving conflicts which you can to some extents gauge or prepare for. However, you will not always have this luxury. Oftentimes the conflict will come out of nowhere and force you to deal with it immediately. So what do you do then?

The answer is simple – use martial arts; specifically any one of the fighting styles which teach you not to fight back with force. Instead use your opponent's aggression and force against him; so every time your opponent attacks you, you dodge him or use some technique which forces him to fight through you while leaving you unharmed. Like a man beating the air, he is unable to affect you simply because you refuse to fight back.

Here's the end result of this semi-comical battle – he is flying around, falling down, and wearying himself while you are seamlessly getting out of his way. This is how you fight back. This is your better way.

MASTERS OF CONFLICT AND CONFIDENCE

Believe it or not, this is a common occurrence; that is the unforeseen, immediate event of conflict. For example, I was working as a consultant at a large firm and doing my best to learn the culture of the company. Yet on one fateful occasion I didn't learn so well, as witnessed by a pointed email I received from one of the managers. She was upset with me because she had incorrectly assumed I was attempting to put her in a bad spot per a request I had made.

So what did she do? Unfortunately she went on the attack. Even worse she did it via email.

If you're not aware of it, here's the problem with email and most forms of artificial communications – a negative message will almost always be received 10 times worse than the sender intended it to be taken. Consequently, the receiver often times perceives the email as threatening and a skirmish is already underway.

So what did I do? Instead of focusing on the incorrect assumptions she had made, I looked for the opportunity for good to come out of the conflict. So I reread the email carefully to understand what was really bothering her.

My mind then went back to concerns she had expressed on past conference calls. Then I put 2 and 2 together and figured out what was really going on with her and how I had inadvertently struck a nerve. So after thoughtful consideration, I replied back with a concise email explaining myself, apologizing for any confusion I may have caused, and offering to meet with her in person to discuss further if necessary.

Within minutes she not only replied back with a gracious thank-you email; she also gave me exactly what I had asked for in the beginning. Moreover, she became one of my biggest supporters while I worked for her firm and is now one of my many friends.

All's well that ends well, so they say and I concur. Yet I would ask each reader to consider an alternate scenario in which I did not handle the conflict well; rather I became defensive and fought back. Do you believe the situation would have ended as well in this development? I think not.

Sadly this alternate scenario transpires all the time and is why so many companies, organizations, and families are filled with divisions and marred by infighting. It's because hardly anyone is willing to be the bigger person in the face of conflict, which is why it hardly ever ends well. All it does is cause immense suffering while closing the door on a great deal of potential.

So here's the million-dollar question – how are you going to succeed where others have failed? How are you going to become a master at handling conflict when it will likely be one of the most difficult things you ever do?

Needless to say, there are many crucial factors in this endeavor. Yet none are more crucial than confidence. See if you are confident in yourself and in your role in any matter, you will not be overly threatened by any false accusations or attacks against your character. It really is that simple.

So someone calls you out. So someone sends you a pointed email. So someone makes derogatory remarks about your person. So what? If these remarks are not true, what do these slanders have to do with you? Exactly; they don't have anything to do with you. They have everything to do with the one who is slandering.

So don't worry about what they're saying. Worry about how you are going to respond, for your response is going to go a much longer way in determining the end result of the conflict than your opponent's initial denigration.

Therefore, in all occasions, be the bigger person; especially when you are. All you have to do is tap into your advanced measures of self-confidence, take a deep breath, and employ the art of fighting without fighting – and I promise you, one way or the other, you will come out on top. The masters of conflict and confidence always do.

THE SUMMATION

Confidence is the foundation of the Pinnacle of Purpose. Accordingly, the first step you take on your path to fulfillment requires you to believe in yourself and your ability to accomplish every purpose you were destined to fulfill.

Along the way, you're going to run into a sad cast of characters who are going to resort to throwing stones at you. Whatever you do, don't fight back. Rather learn the art of fighting without fighting and never concede the high ground. In doing so, you will always be the bigger person and eventually become a master of conflict and confidence.

All the same, you can not afford to be overconfident. You were designed to achieve specific goals, so stay in your lane and don't try to be someone you're not. Believe me; there is no reward in this act, for it represents one of several paths in life which leads nowhere.

As for the path which leads to your destiny, it can only be traveled by you. Be encouraged by this. Be invigorated by it. My dear friends, be excited about the fact that there is a seat in the world classroom with your name on it that only you can sit in.

So get comfortable in your own chair and be comfortable in your own skin. The world needs you as much as it needs anyone else. So be confident and be yourself. This brings me to my final word on confidence.

> **You can achieve any objective in your quest for fulfillment if you have confidence in yourself and your ability to do those things you were designed to do. The key is you were destined to do them, so don't let anyone convince you that you can't. You can, and if you stay on this path you surely will.**

CHAPTER 7

Knowledge

*

*"Of all the things which you must know; above all
else you must know you; And do those things which
help you grow, and to thyself thou must be true."*

BE TRUE TO YOURSELF

Moving on, the second level of the Pinnacle of Purpose is knowledge. Strategically, after gaining the confidence to believe in yourself and your destiny, you must identify your life purposes. This begins with intimately coming to know who you are, from your strengths to your truest desires.

Knowledge is first and foremost important because failure to know yourself intimately is the easiest way to become lost on the path to fulfillment – and as you are unsuccessfully attempting to follow a path which is not pointing towards your destiny, everything you eventually attain in life will never be in full. Rather they will be in part and difficult to consistently enjoy.

Earlier this year I wrote an article for a local magazine entitled, *"Know Yourself."* In this piece I discussed the importance of personal discovery borrowing from the illustrious phrase "man, know thyself and to thine own self be true," an ancient aphorism founded upon the tenets of confidence.

Fundamentally this proverb should be viewed as a teacher's admonition against overconfidence and self-doubt, 2 deficits which not only evolve in line with others' faulty perceptions of you; they are both most effectively resolved by knowledge. As such, this phrase is clearly an appeal for each of us to be who we are no matter how we think others are going to receive us.

This is precisely why many sages caution all to, "pay no attention to the opinion of the multitude;" for as I said before, the world is filled with cynics who are unfortunately as empty as they are shallow. Do you really want to spend one second of your day trying to be accepted by these characters when they haven't even figured out how to accept themselves? Trust me; this is a poor investment, for they can no more accept you than pigs can fly.

Therefore, it is important for you to accept who you are as this is the only manner in which you can continually be yourself without any reservations. This is what many great philosophers and teachers meant when they encouraged their students to be true to themselves. They were urging them to always be themselves in every situation as this is the prevailing validation of knowledge.

THE TIME IS YOURS

Noticeably this level of authenticity and personal loyalty is the ultimate aim of knowledge – and to achieve this superlative grade of honesty, you must first and foremost set aside time for personal discovery. This is crucial because it is impossible to know someone if you don't invest time in getting to know them. This is especially the case for your own self, for how can you truly know who you are if you are constantly out of touch with *you*?

Here lies one of the greatest challenges of 21ˢᵗ century living. The world we live in is arguably more complex than it has ever been. It also moves at a more rapid pace than ever before; specifically from the perspective of our global society. Accordingly, it doesn't matter who you are in life; whether you're a business man, a college student, or a stay-at-home mom, the vast majority of us do not have a surplus of time. On the contrary, many of us have so many things on our plate that we often carry over various initiatives from week to week. Thus we are continually behind and leaving numerous enterprises undone.

The greatest of these is sure – we are striking out with regards to our own personal discovery. If you recall in the introduction, I revealed that this book would be dedicated to helping each reader unlock the greatest mystery in life (i.e. the mystery of you). At this time I would state that the most fundamental step in this process is setting aside time in your already-busy schedule for personal discovery.

See although you have hundreds of matters to attend to and only 168 hours in a week to address them, you must be willing to give yourself a healthy portion of those hours – and why not? After all, the time is yours. It doesn't belong to your boss, your significant other, your friends, or even your children. Your time belongs to you. So ask yourself this question – what kind of person am I if I can't even give myself a few hours each week to make sure I am first and foremost taking care of me?

STAY IN TOUCH WITH YOURSELF

I think I have a pretty good case here. In another life I may have even been a pretty good lawyer. So let's talk about things you can do to enhance your personal discovery beginning with keeping a journal.

Traditionally I love the idea of keeping a journal because we are always changing. Thus from one year to the next you will always be a different person, for what is life but an unbroken chain of personal evolutions?

If you think otherwise I'm somewhat sorry to break it to you, but the person you will become tomorrow is not the person you are today. One way or the other you're going to change. Due to countless events directly and indirectly impacting our lives, none of us will ever remain the same.

This is where a journal comes in. It is one of the best ways (if not the best) to track the "evolutions of you." In doing so, it allows you to see firsthand how you have grown and developed in so many areas – and most importantly, it helps you track your progress upon your path to fulfillment.

All things considered, writing in a journal faithfully does require a healthy amount of time and a unique individual willing to put pen to paper (or fingers to computer keyboard). Maybe that individual is not you. In that case I would advise you to write a list of all your life purposes and keep it some place where you won't forget; say your refrigerator.

Following, review this list from time to time and make sure your time is properly aligned with these purposes. In essence, if you're a father, make sure you're spending a healthy amount of time with your children. If you're a student, make sure you're spending a healthy amount of time studying and doing your best in school.

You get the idea. There are various activities you can do regularly on this wise. Find what works for you while remembering the ultimate goal is to stay in touch with yourself.

Furthermore, do not forget that you are evolving every day. Therefore your personal discovery never truly ends. Neither should any of the enterprises you have established to make sure you never lose touch with the most important person in your life – you.

ESTABLISHING YOUR LIFE PURPOSES

So we've talked about staying true to yourself as well as staying committed to your own personal discovery. At this time we should discuss the 3rd and final high-level objective in the course of knowledge; that is establishing your life purposes. To this end I have identified 10 key questions which will guide you in this endeavor. They are as follows:

1. **What do I enjoy doing more than anything in the world?**
2. **What am I really good at?**
3. **What do I daydream about?**
4. **What are the most important things in life?**
5. **Who are the most important people in my life?**
6. **What do I want my life to be about?**
7. **What are the truest desires of my heart?**
8. **What are the things in life which I can't live without?**
9. **What kind of things would I be happy doing for years to come?**
10. **What does my perfect life look like?**

Now you will make an amazing discovery after answering the first 9 questions; namely there will be 5-8 answers which consistently repeat themselves. Naturally these answers correspond to your life purposes.

As for the 10th question, it should be a short but decisive narrative which captures these purposes. For example, if your answers to these questions reveal your life purposes are being a father, a husband, a police man, and a member of various local institutions, you will need to spell out these purposes with some degree of detail to understand the commitments involved with each office while ensuring each office gets an appropriate allocation of your time.

Besides a brief summary, you will also need to create a strategy for achieving every objective associated with your established life purposes. Like me, you're going to have to become the man (or woman) with the plan. All you have to do is effectively connect all the dots on your roadmap of life, something I will show you how to do as we speak to the remaining levels of the Pinnacle of Purpose.

THE IMMENSE VALUE OF REFLECTION

Now there are various realities which will hit you after you've established your life purposes and created a plan for achieving them. One of these is the fact that your life purposes are likely going to be to some degree a surprise, for many of us only know ourselves in part. This knowledge deficit becomes crystal clear when we ask ourselves a couple of decisive questions and reflect upon our answers.

I was talking with a group of young people several years ago during a workshop geared to help them discover their life purposes. I spent the first 15 minutes asking each member of the group what they felt their life purposes were and was amazed at how confident the group as a whole felt about their answers. They knew what they wanted out of life and most of them already had a pretty good strategy for making it happen – so they thought.

After we finished getting everyone's prospective destinies on the table, I gave them a worksheet with the 10 questions I introduced in the prior section and told them to fill out the first 9 questions. Then 1-by-1 we compared each group member's original answers to the ones which were on their papers.

The results were astounding. See the majority of the class's answers from my worksheet were different than their original responses which we had written on the blackboard. Conclusively there are 2 primary reasons why this was the case.

First of all, the group's original responses were not reflective of their true selves. On the contrary, they were more reflective of pop culture and societal norms. For this cause, the vast majority of their original responses were reflective of varying transitory models representing individuals they thought they were supposed to be per the views and influences of their peers, parents, and others within their societies. They were not representative of the unique individuals they were destined to be.

This matter speaks to the second case; specifically, no one spent any time reflecting on their truest desires and motivations before providing their original answers. That's why my worksheet of 10 questions was so critical in this exercise, for it forced the group to think about their true selves and what they really wanted out of life as opposed to what they thought life had in store for them. Consequently, every group member was able to distinguish their true purposes in life while realizing the immense value of reflection.

WHEN THE LONG WAY IS THE RIGHT WAY

Notwithstanding, this exercise did not necessarily convince the group as a whole that they should pursue their reflective purposes even though they understood it was their destiny to do so. This was primarily because many of them were having difficulty perceiving how they would fulfill their life purposes in light of their individual realities.

Now I initially thought they were lacking self-confidence. Yet as I began to dig deeper, I realized this was not the issue. The issue was much more complicated; explicitly, certain members in the group had realities which were so difficult that some of their life purposes seemed almost impossible to fulfill.

Truth be told, I am a very optimistic person. I've been that way since I was maybe 4. Thus calling me a "glass half-full" man would be untrue. I'm what you would call a "glass almost-full" man. I'm always looking for the good in people and expecting the best to come out of every situation; specifically because I have a solid spiritual foundation and support system.

However, after hearing some of the realities of various group members, my glass almost-full perspective was greatly challenged. For example, there was a young woman in the group whose primary purpose in life was to be a nurse. All signs pointed to it. She was a consummate nurturer and had both the intelligence and work ethic to excel in college.

Yet she was also a member of a broken family. Most notably she had no father figure in her life. This forced her mother to work multiple jobs to support their family.

This also forced the young woman to spend much of her time helping in raising her 5 brothers and sisters after school instead of investing the time necessary to fulfill her purpose of becoming a nurse. Sadly this is just a high-level account of her difficult reality.

So what was I to say to her? What candid advice could I provide? After all, my entire message is predicated upon the fact that everyone has a fair shot at fulfilling their destiny. How was I going to honestly convey this message to her in light of the immense adversity surrounding her life?

Most of us do not like to go off the cuff. Yet this time I was forced to. I did so by initially letting her know she could reach her destiny in spite of her demanding reality.

Predictably she asked me how. So I went on to discuss all the various options she had, none of which were easy apart from some major change in her family life. Neither did they allow her to reach her destiny as quickly as if she were in a better situation.

I'll never forget how my answer seemingly caused her spirit to fail – and why not? Was this fair? Not at all; it was the farthest thing from fair and I let her know that, for it was imperative for me to establish some form of common ground and credibility now that the conversation was leaning towards the unproductive view of misfortunes and the lamentable misunderstandings which tend to follow.

I then went on to remind the group of a harsh reality; that is minorities (e.g. racial, social, physically handicapped, etc.), women, and their advocates have championed countless efforts over hundreds of years in the order of making life "more fair."

I also reminded them that even though we still have a ways to go, we are much farther along than we have ever been. To this they agreed, so I asked them why they felt we were much farther along.

To be expected, they knew the answer. It's because countless world heroes have dedicated their lives to numerous progressive causes which have systematically changed our world for the better.

From there we went on to discuss many great men and women in history who fought for freedom and against injustice in our country and around the world. Then we talked about how hard it must have been for them to champion such difficult but necessary causes; especially for those who lost their lives fighting and standing up for their beliefs.

After considering these factors I asked them pointedly, "Did these great men and women fulfill their destinies? In spite of the tremendous toil they endured and the fact that some of them were murdered unjustly, did these world heroes indeed live a life of purpose?"

Everyone looked around the room, deliberated for a short while, and then agreed that these illustrious men and women had indeed fulfilled their destiny. So I asked them if they knew why this was true.

Again they all looked around the room at each other and discussed their thoughts for a small while. Yet they were unable to come to a consensus on this matter. That's when they asked me what my thoughts were. So I told them, "It's true because of me and because of all of you." In essence, everyone in that room regardless of race, gender, religion, or any other social descriptor, was a beneficiary of every great man and woman who had successfully fulfilled their destiny.

After a very heartfelt and emotional discourse, I turned to the young woman whose destiny to be a nurse prompted the discussion and said, "Your path may not be as easy as some who go to better schools and have more resources at their disposal, but I promise you this – if you stay the course and live your life with purpose, it will be even more rewarding.

Moreover, and like those who came before you who allowed you to have opportunities none of your ancestors had, you are going to open doors for your children and grandchildren to have opportunities you didn't have simply by fulfilling your destiny."

A smile finally came to her face as she looked at me and nodded. We made a connection then and there. The entire group did. See even though we came to the conclusion that life isn't fair (and on the whole may never be), we were committed to operating in the feted model of some of the greatest men and women of all time.

In doing so, we refused to focus on the unfair realities of life. On the contrary, we were determined to focus on what mattered most; that would be fulfilling our destiny by any means necessary, and becoming original heroes of our world.

I'll never forget that red-letter day and how I had truly learned more from my group than they had learned from me. Then again, I'll never forget how I determined one of my greatest core values as a result of this discourse. The value – we must always be committed to taking the long way when it is the right way.

THE SUCCESS YOU ARE TRULY SEEKING

Another reason why some members in the group had trouble accepting their destiny is because they were putting more stock in achieving success as opposed to fulfillment. As a result, they were more inclined to follow the unrealistic paradigms of society as opposed to their truest desires.

For instance, I met a young man who had originally said his primary life purpose was to be a professional basketball player. However, after going through my worksheet, he determined that his primary life purpose was to be a teacher. Like me, one of his truest passions in life was helping people via education. His profile confirmed the rest. This young man was destined to be an educator.

In his heart he knew this; which is partly why he wanted to be a professional athlete, for this more visible occupation would potentially allow him to have a greater platform to help others. He even cited examples of various athletes who execute a profound measure of charitable work, engage in numerous forms of outreach, and meritoriously give back to their communities. Thus, in his mind, all he had to do was be successful as a ball player and the rest would fall into place.

Now even though this was all true, my job was to help this young man realize his truest desire was not necessarily becoming a professional athlete.

It was being in a position where he could help others – and since he was an exceptional student, it was also my responsibility to help him come to the conclusion that it would be more practical for him to initially target professions in which he could fulfill his innate desire to teach. Because he was so receptive to my advice, I was able to do so in short order.

All the same, this didn't mean becoming a professional athlete was off the table. In fact I encouraged him to pursue this dream as long as he felt it was realistic for a sure cause – becoming a professional athlete (especially nowadays) is an immense challenge which will take a great deal of time practicing and honing in on varying physical skills.

Therefore, as the competition is so great and the requirements are so high, it won't take most of us too long to realize whether or not this dream is indeed realistic for us. Truly, so many want to be the next superstar in their sport of choice; yet do they realize how much dedication it takes to even give themselves a shot?

I have a cousin who spent over 10 years as a professional basketball player in the NBA and I'm quite sure he would confirm my position. That's why I encouraged the young man to focus on his studies and his desire to help others first and foremost – and if basketball became something he could excel at without compromising any of his other life purposes, I encouraged him to pursue it. Moreover, I promised him I would come see him play when and if he makes it.

On the other hand, I encouraged him not to feel disappointed if he didn't. As I said before, we all have various roles to fulfill in life, all of which are distinct and can be served better by no one other than us. Therefore, it is important for us to be willing to accept our roles no matter how glamorous they are by society's often backwards standards.

As I told this exceptional young man, "Whether you're a professional basketball player with a large platform or a teacher on a smaller stage, be proud of your role and do your best to be your best in it; for although you may not realize it now, this is the success you are truly seeking."

THE SUMMATION

The most important person in your life is you. Therefore, you must consistently stay in touch with yourself by tracking your personal evolution. You can do this by keeping a journal or by simply managing a list of your priorities. Whatever you decide to do, be sure to do this one thing – never lose touch with you.

Furthermore, if you ever come to a point in your life where you're not quite sure what you should be doing, ask yourself the 10 critical questions found in the section entitled, *"Establishing Your Life Purposes."* These will help you discover (or rediscover) your life purposes and position you to align your time accordingly. You just have to be willing to accept your destiny no matter how complex the path may be.

Then again you must always bear in mind a crucial reality – life isn't always fair and on the whole it will never be. Inopportunely this has caused many to forfeit their destiny and become victims of fate. Therefore, if you're going to avoid this depressed state, you need to do more than simply discover your life purposes. You must also believe in yourself and your ability to fulfill each one. You learned how to do this during the prior lecture on confidence.

Bearing this in mind, do not allow yourself to be enticed into giving up if certain stretches of your path to fulfillment are tough to follow. Tough as it may be, your destiny is yours. You must own it, and you must do whatever it takes to succeed while always considering the following – the more difficult your path is, the more fulfilling your destiny will be.

Lastly, to resist the ever-present enticement to settle, you must keep yourself from comparing yourself to anyone else; specifically those who you think have it better than you do. Trust me; not everyone who appears to be thriving in life is doing as well as you think they are. As the saying goes – all that glitters isn't gold.

Moreover, how would you know whether or not someone is truly thriving or well-off? The only path which offers you enduring success is your own individual path to fulfillment. Therefore, as there is no value in trying to decipher the path of another, stay committed to discovering your own path and follow it all the way to the top of your personal pinnacle of purpose. This brings me to my final word on knowledge.

It is impossible to perceive the path to your destiny if you do not first come to know who you are and consistently remain in touch with you. So man, know thyself and to thine own self be true.

CHAPTER 8

Judgment

*

"It's hard to make a choice in life, for fear of that
which we should lose; Yet we must judge the wrong
from right, and in the end we all must choose."

WHY MANY NEVER FULFILL THEIR DESTINY

The third level of the Pinnacle of Purpose is judgment. Strategically the objective of judgment is to gain the ability to consistently make the right choices in life (i.e. choices which are aligned with your destiny). This is crucial for a sure cause which I will offer as an early interest point in this lecture.

> **The quality of your life is measured by the quality of your choices.**

This is clearly evident, for every decision we make corresponds to a step. The key to living a life of purpose, then, is to make sure our choices in life correspond to the steps on our path to fulfillment.

All things considered, our lives will not necessarily begin spiraling out of control if we make a choice which is not on our path to fulfillment. Quite the opposite; the consequences of many of these choices (rather mistakes) are neither permanent nor immediate. Yet some of them are.

This speaks to the vast significance of judgment, for whether or not poor judgment causes us to fail in our quest after a series of mistakes or just one is inconsequential. On the whole, poor judgment is the primary reason why many never fulfill their destiny, for the collective impact of the ensuing mistakes will be too great for these to recover from them.

With regards to the path to fulfillment, these will have taken too many wrong turns – and as they've gotten so far removed from the beaten path, it is highly unlikely that they should ever return. Sadly very many will never fulfill their destiny for this cause alone.

DETERMINED TO OVERCOME

It's tragic enough seeing individuals gradually migrate away from a life of purpose. It's even more tragic when someone falls away in a single turn by making a poor choice. Unfortunately I've seen this tragic tale much too often in my life.

Now I was raised in the church and, once upon a time, I revered church-goers above all others. This was especially the case for an extraordinary young woman.

I was in my early teens at the time. She was a straight-A student, beyond likeable, fine-looking, and one of the most respected members of our youth group. Everyone looked up to her as one of the brightest young persons in the entire community.

Then one day she fatefully met a man several years her senior. Yet this did not stop him from pursuing her. Within a few months she was pregnant and her life would change forever.

Now I watched her fairly closely to see how it would impact her because I cared for her as my friend and I had compassion on her – and it made me thoroughly upset to see so many others judging her unrighteously. See all the losers who hated on her before because of her goodness were the first ones to rise up in judgment against her after this poor decision. In the words of Mark Twain, "That's life as I know it."

Sad to say and sadder still, the first year after this episode was difficult for her. She missed some time from school, went through the difficult process of giving birth as a high school student; the list goes on.

Nevertheless, the difficult nature of her situation didn't destroy her. As a matter of fact, I believe it made her stronger; for in spite of the increased difficulty in her life, she eventually graduated from high school and then went on to obtain multiple college degrees. Currently she has both a successful career and marriage.

So in the end and after all, her former error in judgment didn't destroy her willingness to yet pursue and fulfill her destiny. It may have caused some trying setbacks and increased the complexity of her quest, but her determination was greater than the sum of her challenges and propelled her every step of a more difficult, yet possibly even more satisfying way.

This is why she is one of my life heroines. She is the epitome of one of the greatest lessons in life; namely, you can overcome any unwise decision you make if you are truly determined to overcome.

WHEN ALL IT TAKES IS ONE

Nonetheless, I would have to classify this story as an exception to this crucial rule. The sad truth is that many of the women I know who became pregnant as young teenagers (and were unwed or did not wed the father) are not heroines of perfect success stories. On the contrary, they are the objects of tragic accounts of unlimited potential unfulfilled.

On one such occasion, a bright young lady fell into the same situation as the heroine in the preceding story. However, she did not possess the same resolve. Instead she became depressed and eventually had another child.

Later she dropped out of high school. She then went through several episodes of domestic violence with the father of her children. One such episode almost killed her.

Without going further into her narrative, I would state a very heart-rending fact; that is this young lady is extremely bright and yet full of potential. However, all of this great potential remains unfulfilled for one reason – she has never recovered from one bad decision. Rather she has compounded the situation with continued erroneous judgment and additional poor choices.

Still these are not the issue and would never even have been if she had resisted the temptation to take one step outside of her purpose (which at that point in time shouldn't have been much more than graduating from high school and fulfilling her limited roles in life). The issue here is the devastation one mistake can potentially cause.

So remember this as you are on your quest for fulfillment and are enticed to engage in perilous acts dripping with temporary pleasures. Remember that it doesn't take multiple errors to exponentially increase the obscurity of your quest for fulfillment. All it takes is one.

THE MORAL COMPASS

Going further, there are major differences between those who continually make poor decisions and those who are tragically impacted by a single mistake. First of all, those who consistently make bad choices are almost always without excuse for the following cause – everyone has a moral compass which is unbroken in its origin. In essence, it points to true you and will lead you along the path of fulfillment, a path marked by righteous decisions.

As for the repeat offender, he or she will purposefully override the direction given to them by their moral compass and willfully go down paths they know are wrong. Here's what they do not realize – the majority of those who have traveled these broken paths have yet to recover, and some of them will never return. Alas, they rose to play with fire; yet failed to consider how they would eventually get burned.

So how does this person become a repeat offender? Here's the answer – the fallout from a bad decision is not always immediate. Thus the severest consequences of poor judgment are often delayed.

Moreover, they can be avoided altogether if the individual in question makes one of the wisest decisions of all time; that is learning from a mistake without suffering the full breadth of the consequences (the former model is often referred to as "dodging a bullet" while the latter is denoted as learning the hard way).

Unfortunately many don't appreciate these sentiments. So instead of getting it together and executing a much needed course-correction in response to the direction provided to them by their moral compass, they double-down on poor judgment and continue to travel further and further away from their path to fulfillment.

Devastatingly a byproduct of this continued poor decision-making is the compromising of one's moral compass, for your moral compass is in some way damaged every time you make a bad decision – and the only way to remedy this damage is to correct the mistake you made and learn from it. Otherwise your moral compass will become compromised and no longer point to true you.

Classically this is the primary reason why so many become lost on the crossroads of life while finding themselves in the image of a man or woman they were never supposed to be. Their moral compass is broken and is leading them down paths they never intended to go. This ultimately causes them to become someone they're not while steadily decreasing the prospects that they should ever fulfill their purpose.

This matter lends itself to the most fitting model of poor judgment. It is a patented slippery slope; for once you start down this path, it gets gradually harder to regain your footing. Accordingly, the likelihood of you making a bad decision increases exponentially when you continue to employ poor judgment – and there is a point of no return in this process.

YOU ALWAYS HAVE A CHOICE

I am a huge promoter of non-profit organizations for many progressive reasons. As a matter of fact, one of the primary goals of Life Pinnacles is to provide increased visibility to the non-profit world. This is contingent to the fact that I created Life Pinnacles as an extension of the non-profit community; albeit we target clients and members throughout various social and professional outlets.

Now of all the non-profit groups and initiatives, I spend more time supporting domestic violence coalitions for this cause – many victims of domestic violence are also victims of the aforementioned model of poor judgment. Therefore, they are severely in need of the message of purpose; specifically the tenets of confidence, knowledge, and judgment.

However, unlike those who make bad decisions for inexcusable reasons, many victims of domestic violence are in this model for justifiable causes and are unable to get out of their difficult situations alone. This is why thousands like me are advocates of this social crisis.

Now although victims of domestic violence come in all shapes and sizes, I would like to concentrate primarily on female victims during this lecture; particularly women who are married or in some way involved with their abuser (i.e. physically or emotionally).

In my experience, most domestic violence victims have no idea at the outset that the man they love or are with will ever act against them violently. Believe me; I've heard the personal accounts of countless women and their initial sentiments about the man of their dreams are similar if not the same. On the whole, this man could hardly do wrong in their eyes; that is until the first incident of domestic violence.

Now before moving forward into this discussion, I would like to submit the following admission – the issue of domestic violence is one of the most sensitive social issues. Therefore I, being merely an advocate as opposed to an expert, will not offer my opinions about the core matters of such a delicate subject matter. Neither will I, in this section or this composition, attempt to resolve this issue in any order. Yet I will speak to my knowledge with regards to the corresponding factor of poor judgment and the role it plays in each ill-fated incident of domestic violence.

I would begin by stating one of my strongest beliefs – a good wife is the most precious gift a man will ever receive, followed closely by his children. This being the case I ask – would a good man ever act violently towards the most precious gift he has ever acquired? I think not. Thus for that reason alone, any man who acts violently towards his woman or his children is not (by my personal standards) a good man; period, end of story.

Now the first critical moment in situations of domestic violence is how the woman responds after the initial incident. Whether she stays or leaves is not necessarily the most important thing. The most important thing is that she does not justify or make an excuse for his violence.

I believe this because I have heard the stories of women who blamed themselves for their man's violence. See this is a mistake; for even if the woman is at fault for some facet of the episode, it is never her fault when she is forced to endure any episode of violence.

All things considered, this doesn't necessarily mean every abuser is wholly evil or a lost cause. The unfortunate reality is that many young men don't have responsible father figures in their lives. As a consequence, they often enter into intimate relationships with various personal deficits and flaws; specifically the inability to handle conflict in a productive manner.

Undesirably this is why some men will resort to violence. It's because they don't know how to effectively deal with conflict. Likewise they've never been taught how to resist the faulty temptation to fight back; in particular with force.

If I had to venture I would surmise nearly 8 out of every 10 offenders fall into this depressing model. Be that as it may, my wife taught and regularly reminds me of a crucial reality; explicitly, no matter what life throws at you, you always have a choice with regards to how you are going to deal with it.

Observably this is where the rubber meets the road. See it doesn't matter what others may have done to you or how irresponsible or ill-advised parents may have set you back. At the end of the day you always have a choice to make, and nobody can make that choice but you.

This goes back to poor judgment, for it's always a bad decision to mistreat your most precious possessions. Someone who does so is clearly having issues with their moral compass. The question is – what do they do?

EMOTIONS AND THE DECISION-MAKING PROCESS

Let's talk about the woman in this hypothetical scenario. First and foremost she should put distance between herself and the offender. This is good judgment and the best decision she could possibly make at this juncture because one of the most sacred lines in a marriage has been crossed.

Although it is often disregarded and regretfully (yet habitually) considered unofficial as it pertains to cultural and sadly religious norms, this line is domestic violence. Once it has been crossed, the relationship for all intents and purposes will never be the same. The question is – can the relationship be saved?

Honestly it depends on the ensuing choices which are made after the woman removes herself from the violence. These choices should be based upon her desire and willingness to trust the man again predicated on the reality that her trust must increase as a result of the violence – and if she can't bring herself to these higher levels of trust, she shouldn't return to the relationship. Undoubtedly this would be a bad decision.

As straightforward as this matter is, this clear path is generally not taken because women are by nature emotional creatures; usually much more emotional than men. Accordingly, their emotions will often be a factor in their decision-making process. Thus their emotional connection with their offender will often cause them to return to him even though he is likely in no better position than he was before she left. Regardless of this fact many women will return to the situation prematurely.

Needless to say, the results of these actions will often result in additional acts of domestic violence simply because the associative deficits are still intact – and as the best indicator for future behavior is past behavior, the offender will almost always act in the same manner again if he has not resolved his issues at the source.

ESTABLISH YOUR BOUNDARIES AND NEVER SETTLE

Now although this matter is simple at this extremely high level, making the right decision for many women (and men) is extremely difficult. Besides the emotional connection they often have with their offender, there are other factors which add to the complication of this matter. All in all the recovery process is not going to be easy. This brings us to another interest point.

> **Customarily, making the right choices in life is extremely difficult and a challenge within and of itself.**

Ask yourself this question – is being alone easy? I don't think so; especially if you've spent a good portion of your life living with someone else. Nevertheless, being alone still represents the better of 2 difficult worlds; for being alone (which is by no means permanent) is a lot better (and safer) than remaining in an abusive relationship. The question is – how do we get women in this situation to realize this?

Decisively it begins with empowering them to make the right choices in this and every other area of their life. Strategically I accomplish this by utilizing the model of the Pinnacle of Purpose. As we have already stated, the first step in this process is having confidence, a character trait which many women in this situation severely lack. So whenever I have the opportunity to talk to these women, the first thing I do is work to build up their confidence. Explicitly, I work with them to establish boundaries with regards to what is acceptable behavior with regards to their well-being and what is not.

I was talking to a group of young women years ago on this wise. The first thing I had them do was make positive statements about themselves.

This activity worked to remind them of how beautiful, special, and precious they were as young women.

After getting them into this positive mood and reinforcing how they were all exquisite treasures, I asked them a direct question inquiring, "Seeing as you are so valuable and your price above rubies, how should you be treated by the man you love?"

They then went on to describe (in fantastic terms and without constraint) how they felt they should be handled by the man of their dreams.

Now I was very excited to see how they were setting extremely high yet reasonable standards; standards which reflected on their true value as beautiful young women. Besides this, I was excited to see that they were intrigued by this exercise; likely because no one regularly asked them how they wanted to be treated. Consequently, they had lost touch with this crucial requirement and were positioning themselves to be treated below their truest standards.

After we completed the exercise, I drew a circle around all the standards these young women had set for themselves and declared, "This, ladies, is your personal boundary. If any man makes it known to you that he loves you and wants to be with you in any way, you make sure he is aware of this boundary and you never settle."

A FEW GOOD MEN

Now in spite of the sheer validity of this exercise (witnessed by the fact that the women had set their own criteria), many in the group began bailing on me after I reinforced their boundary. Here's why – they weren't convinced there were many (if any) men willing to commit to them according to their authentic values and standards.

First off I informed them that they were making an assumption based upon a generalization of men – and although the conclusion may have been close to accurate, the process by which the conclusion was made was not a successful formula for deliberating or framing a credible hypothesis.

Ultimately this is what they were doing and dangerously, for their contrary perspective (spurred on by their admitted generalities) was situated to compromise their fulfillment. Plainly speaking, their assessment of men in general could potentially cause them to miss out on the man they wanted.

I told them this of course, but they still were not convinced. So I took the next best approach and reassured them that their standards were still more than reasonable even if they may have decreased the pool of potential suitors exponentially.

I even told them I was such a man and I was convinced there were other men out there like me, but that response didn't work very well. See everyone who knows me knows I am (for better or for worse) the exception to almost every social rule. One of my acquaintances frequently refers to me as a "rare breed of man nearing extinction." Another acquaintance jokingly refers to me as a "living legend."

The sad reality is I can not argue with either of them because it's true. From the perspective of a man, my experiences have led me to the following conclusion – even though there are exceptionally good men out there, it often feels like they are few and far in between. Similarly they are sometimes hard to find.

Now I attribute this impression to 2 facts: society often portrays men in a biased manner and a good portion of men are not committed to being themselves. Instead they are often trying to meet some unofficial, unfounded standard which their society has irresponsibly placed on them as men. As a result, both the best and the truth within many men is scarcely seen.

As you would expect, the young women in this class demonstrably reminded me of this (in so many terms). Therefore, seeing as I had already conceded this particular argument, I had to make the conversation about them (i.e. the ladies) and not the limited pool of a few good men.

I did so by asking them the following question – are you willing to wait for the right man who you were destined to be with or will you settle for something less?

I'll never forget how quiet the room became after I asked this question. All the excitement disappeared as everyone became very serious as they pondered over my inquiry. See although these young women knew what the man of their dreams looked like, they were faced with the difficult reality that there was no telling when he would show up.

The grim question which followed was sure – if he took longer than they were prepared to wait, would they be able to resist the persistent temptation to settle for less? Did they have the resolve to make the difficult choice to stay true to themselves while holding fast to their authentic values?

One of my preferred sayings suggests the best things come to those who wait. Those who adhere to this example will always use good judgment, for they realize the great peril associated with settling in any matter. Thus settling should never be an option; for when you begin to compromise your truest standards, you begin compromising you.

THE FUTURE IS UNTOUCHED

Here's what it all comes down to – many of us are or have been in situations marred by poor judgment. If this is where you are at in your life, you must do whatever it takes to stop this slide; even get another party involved.

Perhaps you don't want to tell someone close to you. I understand that; so tell someone you don't know. There are non-profit groups all over the world who have trained professionals who know how to deal with your unique situation. Get in contact with them. Let them help you find your way back to a life of purpose and reclaim the wonderful destiny which still has your name on it.

My dear friends, reclaim the life you are still able to have if you're willing to commit yourself to making good decisions. You can do this. The only question is – are you finally ready to stop settling or will you continue to wander in a valley void of fulfillment?

Believe me; at the end of the day it doesn't matter if the road to your destiny isn't a perfect walk in the park highlighted by you and your loved ones picking daisies. Let's face it. Life is not easy. No one walks through it completely unscathed. So on the whole what matters most is not how relaxed your life is. What matters most is fulfilling your purpose.

So don't let anyone tell you your life is over because you've made a crucial mistake or have been in a bad situation for an extended period of time. Most of these individuals are detractors who are failing in their own life and have sadly resorted to throwing stones.

Remember – you can use these stones for your good. All you have to do is turn their slanders into progressive challenges which allow you to gradually remove yourself from your current position back onto the path to fulfillment.

Then again, never forget this enduring truth – the future is untouched and is waiting for you to make the most of it. So do not dwell on the past, for it is a certain matter which we can not change. Instead use the past constructively by converting it into a series of lessons to help you determine those things which you should do and those which you should not. Brothers and sisters, use your past to build your future, one good decision at a time.

THE SUMMATION

Fundamentally life is all about making choices. The right choices will lead you down your path to fulfillment. The wrong choices will take you off this path and lead you farther away from your destiny. Thus the summation of this chapter is simply this – choose wisely.

Remember this also – all it takes is one mistake to cripple your prospects of fulfillment in the most devastating way. Additionally there are mistakes in life which offer no potential for recovery. So again I caution you to choose wisely.

What is more, you must be committed to following the direction provided by your moral compass. One of the most critical pieces in your quest, your moral compass points directly to your destiny. Thus as long as you follow it, you will make the right decisions.

Nevertheless, it is highly unlikely that you are going to go through life making the right decision in every situation. Like everyone else in the world, you are going to make some mistakes. Don't be discouraged by this. 99% of these mistakes are not going to keep you from your destiny; albeit they will to some degree make your path more difficult.

Heretofore, the most important aspect of judgment is not whether or not you are going to make a mistake. The most important aspect of judgment is your determination to overcome every mistake you will have made. This brings me to the final word on judgment.

The only manner in which you can overcome an occasion of bad judgment is by displaying good judgment. In doing so, you will own up to your mistakes and, in parallel, right the ship.

CHAPTER 9

Work Ethic

*

"A preacher came to me to tell, a tale of how the weary fell; Who were to hope as some wouldst sell, the water from an empty well."

MORE THAN WORKING HARD

The fourth level of the Pinnacle of Purpose is work ethic. This should not be difficult to understand after going through our lessons on judgment. From these we determined that making the right choices in life will always require more effort than making the wrong ones. Accordingly, if we are to consistently display good judgment, we must develop sound work ethic.

Now first things first; developing sound work ethic is not equated to simply working hard. Therefore, I will submit an applicable definition of this focal level of purpose.

Sound work ethic is an efficient work style which allows us to effectively fulfill all of our life purposes by consciously and regularly ensuring our efforts are balanced throughout our life offices.

Definitively the key to developing sound work ethic is balance. As we all have multiple life offices, we must be focused on excelling in each one.

Less our failure to live a balanced life will have a negative impact on each of our life offices, for they are all connected and impacted by each other.

This is especially the case for our professional careers; specifically because they usually represent the life office which causes us to fail to achieve balance in our lives if we should fail. Consequently, the failure of many to effectively manage their professional careers is the primary reason why they do not have sound work ethic. Instead these individuals will almost always become workaholics who will fatefully move further and further away from their path to fulfillment.

All the same, I'm not encouraging anyone to slack when it comes to any of their careers (professional or social). See I'm a big fan of hard work. Yet I'm an even bigger fan of balance because it allows us to channel our desire to work hard in the most efficient manner.

Here's the conclusion of this matter – as our professional careers are usually the greatest threats to achieving balance (and ultimately fulfillment), we must consistently ensure that we are not falling into the unproductive model of a workaholic. Else we will surely incur setbacks in our other life offices and fail to progress our quest for fulfillment.

WHAT'S YOUR ASKING PRICE?

I can speak to this matter because I've seen it firsthand. One of my closest friends has a father who is a patented workaholic and has been one as long as we can remember, a tragic situation which has prevented them from having any kind of reckonable relationship. To this day he often tells me that he still doesn't know his father and since his father (we'll refer to him as Mr. J) is yet determined to live a life of imbalance, he probably never will.

Now even though Mr. J's lack of balance has had obvious negative consequences on his family, I'm quite sure his lack of balance has been appreciated by his employers simply because they benefited the most from it. As they got more out of him than anyone else, I seriously doubt they had any issue with the fact that Mr. J has been "missing in action" as a father, grandfather, and in other social offices.

I would even conjecture that they (i.e. his employers) marveled at him and said to themselves, "Wow! Here's a man who'll work countless hours, sacrifice relationships, essentially do whatever it takes for this job. We have to do everything within our power to keep him and make him feel good about selling out to us. Mark him down as a corporate keeper!"

As you would expect, that's exactly what they did. They offered Mr. J enough physical benefits to keep him focused on individual success that he, over time, became completely oblivious to the fact that the path he was on was void of fulfillment. This brings us to a crucial interest point on work ethic.

> **One of the greatest temptations on the quest for fulfillment is overdoing it in our life offices which are highly depicted by financial success.**

Notwithstanding, there are 2 important facets about this model of success which we touched on briefly during Chapter 4; both of which are crucial to this lecture on work ethic.

First of all, the benefits associated with this transitory model of success will never last; for success apart from fulfillment is incomplete, and (as we stated beforehand) every path demarcated by individual success concludes with a dead-end. Thus how *successful* will we be devoting our time to a model which will eventually fail?

Secondly, this manner of success will always come at a price. This is the second half of the story which many do not consider when they sell out to their professional careers or any other life office. Alas, if you read the fine print on this idiomatic can of worms, this is what you're going to see – you can have all the individual success in life you can handle, but it's going to cost you.

For some it has cost them their families. For others it has cost them their health. What it all comes down to (and what all the enticers in your life are wondering) is this – what is your asking price? What is it going to take to get you to sell out to us so that we can steal the time you should be investing towards your other life purposes and use it for our benefit?

TIMES AND SEASONS

As fate would have it, Mr. J's employers were able to meet his asking price. As a result, he has been the head of a dysfunctional family for years – and although Mr. J may not be directly responsible for every mal-incident within his family, many of these could have been avoided or progressively resolved if Mr. J hadn't been M.I.A. at critical moments in the development of his family office.

Now whether or not Mr. J realized his compromise would yield disastrous consequences is inconsequential. The fact of the matter is that he continues to operate in this model. This is true even though his employers eventually sold him out.

This goes back to my prior assertion that what goes around eventually comes around. Alas, because he was willing to sell out his family and others in favor of his professional career, the corporation which he sold out to repaid him the favor. See fate took one of its unpredictable turns and put this man out of the office he had devoted more time to than all others.

The question I would ask him and those who have similar stories is simply this – was it worth it? You sold out to your job (or some other office) and they in turn sold you out. All of your other life offices have suffered for years and many of them are now dysfunctional. Others have vanished altogether.

If nothing else I guess that's equity. I mean after all, both parties sold out for reasons suitable for a mercenary – and shady as this mode of personal contract may be, the Golden Rule was applied. Karma did prevail. Justice was served. Yet I'm still wondering if it was worth it.

Now another one of my preferred sayings suggests the best way to learn is from other people's mistakes. I take this lesson to heart with specific regards to this example because the only thing worse than being a member of a dysfunctional family is being the head of one.

This is why I take parenting so seriously. It's because I've seen the obvious, adverse effects which follow fathers and mothers who refuse to fulfill their roles in the lives of their children. Therefore, I have taken a personal oath not to allow these events to ever befall my family.

Furthermore, I can make the following assessment – Mr. J's son is enjoying higher levels of fulfillment and success than Mr. J. Certainly I don't make this assertion in an effort to compare them on an isolated scale. Rather I make it to verify my original argument that enduring success must be tied to our personal dedication to effectively managing each of our life offices and striving for balance. For this cause alone, one would have to be disillusioned to presume they're going to obtain the highest measures of success life can offer by neglecting even one purpose which life designed them to fulfill.

Here's another thing – there is a time and a season associated with every progressive pursuit in life which we must follow to obtain the success we are looking for. Ergo, there is a time and a season for every purpose we must fulfill. Therefore, the most critical aspect of life is being sensitive to these appointed times, for we will constantly fail to fulfill our purpose if we are unaware of the times and seasons we are in.

PRIORITIZING YOUR LIFE PURPOSES

After considering all of this information, it should be clear that there is nothing wonderful about being a workaholic; especially because this model is sure-to-fail – and, dare I ask, is there anything wonderful about being a failure?

Now although these will hardly ever admit it, and even so the disastrous results of this ruinous model are not generally manifested overnight, the reality is sure – behind every workaholic is a fragmented man or woman void of fulfillment. Is this how you want your life to unfold? Is this who you want to be?

It's not who I want to be and I assume this to be true for most of us. So let's continue this lecture by further discussing the greatest source of sound work ethic; that would be balance. Accordingly, the question of the hour is simply this – how do you achieve balance?

The answer to this critical question is as simple as it is sure; explicitly, you must be committed to following the plan you created for achieving your life purposes. You created this plan while you were on the level of knowledge and answered 10 critical questions which helped you identify your life purposes.

Although we didn't discuss it at that time, part of this plan involves you prioritizing all of your life purposes. This is important because it will involve determining how much time you need to dedicate to each life office such that you successfully fulfill each of your roles.

After setting reasonable time goals for each office, all you have to do is abide by these goals. This is essentially how you achieve balance, simple enough.

Notwithstanding, taking this proactive approach will not wholly protect you from falling into the seductive model of a workaholic; a model I refer to as such for the following cause – even though a workaholic is one of the least fulfilled and most tragic characters in life, many of them are in part successful; particularly from a monetary perspective.

This speaks to the sad motivations and expectations of many workaholics. For some reason or another they're overly fixated on the accumulation of wealth. This fixation could be one of pure greed or it could evolve from fear of the unknown. Either or, their fixation will position them to become imbalanced.

This is precisely why they will invest inordinate amounts of time in offices yielding high measures of wealth as opposed to other offices such as parenting, mentoring, or community service. Unlike these less affluent offices, overdoing it in those financially-endowed offices has a bounty tied to it and the bounty is usually high.

Still, and as I said before, this transitory pursuit also has a price tag on it – and the price is never cheap. However, many disregard the price and focus solely on the bounty, which is the primary reason why they become workaholics. They've become blinded by wealth and material things or they've allowed for their fears (and a consequent over-emphasis on job security) to become more important than their fulfillment.

NEVER LOSE SIGHT OF WHAT MATTERS MOST

This line of discussion speaks to the aforementioned importance of accepting our destiny and staying focused on our life purposes. In this regard, we don't have to lose sight of all of our life purposes to begin veering off the path to fulfillment. We just have to lose focus on one.

This is another matter I can attest to in my own life. Recall how I became the Director of Consulting Services at one of the largest IT firms in the state of Indiana at 25? Well this was huge. Most professionals spend 10+ years in their industry before they're even considered for such a position. So I was very excited to be an exception to a very strict rule.

However, my excitement about this amazing opportunity began to dwindle in the course of time. Why? You should know the answer by now. See although I didn't recognize it immediately, I was failing in my other life offices.

Let's talk about the family office. My wife and I had 3 small children at the time. So naturally there was an increasing demand for me as a husband and a father to allocate time towards the various causes related to raising a young family.

At the same time, demands at work were also increasing. Including my daily 2-hour commute, I was spending anywhere from 12-14 hours at work daily while working weekends. This had a lot to do with my new role and my desire to be successful in it.

Unsurprisingly this transition didn't faze me in the beginning. It did however faze my wife and for good reason, for my failure to faithfully fulfill my role in the family office was having a negative effect on her ability to fulfill hers. Plainly speaking, she was forced to pick up where I was slacking.

To my good fortune my wife is a very patient woman. She is incredibly more patient than I am. Accordingly, she never pressed me too much on the issue.

Even when she did I was too distracted to realize what she was saying. That's because there's a difference between listening and hearing. Often times you can hear someone and fail to listen because you're distracted. Hence you're not really getting what they are trying to tell you.

Unfortunately that's where I was at. Because I was over-concerned (and over-focused) with succeeding as a director, it became difficult for me to comprehend my wife's concerns; even so they were more legitimate than my reasons for pushing the envelope in my professional career.

So here's what happened – my family life hit an all-time low, the intense work hours caused me to lose 50 pounds, and ultimately I became very ill. It was during that time that the light bulb finally went off. There I realized it was going to be impossible for me to continue on the path I had been on and somehow find fulfillment. At the very least it was because my family was suffering and would continue to suffer as a result of my lack of balance.

Furthermore, even though my career appeared to be a success and was successful in part, my life on the whole was far from successful. It was even farther from fulfilled. Besides this none of my clothes fit me anymore. So I went through the crucial exercise of reestablishing my priorities and working to restore the credibility I had lost in the offices I was clearly behind in.

In the end I lost my director position. Yet this thing did not displease me in any way. As I had regained my focus in life, I knew I could not operate in such a demanding role and remain on the path to fulfillment because of the time and season of life I was in – and I was determined never to lose sight of what mattered most again.

GREAT INVESTMENTS, GREAT REWARDS

Until now we have primarily discussed the perils of poor work ethic with regards to overdoing it in one or more life offices. At this time we should discuss the peril of poor work ethic with regards to those who aren't working hard enough in any of their life offices. This is devastating for several reasons.

To begin with, the path to fulfillment is parallel to another critical path in life; namely the path to excellence. The reason why this path is so critical represents another interest point.

> **It is impossible to walk the path to fulfillment without simultaneously walking the path to excellence.**

Markedly the path to excellence is highlighted by men and women excelling in each of their life offices. Believe you me; this is a more wonderful and remarkable reality than most realize.

To be quite honest I can't even describe it in words. When everyone in a family, a project team, a business unit, or any other social group is on the same page and excelling in their roles, an amazing event occurs — true and matchless fulfillment.

Still the most crucial realization concerning this matter is centered on the fact that fulfillment is impossible to reach apart from excellence. Reason being, fulfillment is the greatest reward we can obtain in life. Therefore, it will require our greatest investment.

I refer to this principle as the *"Investment Principle."* It reveals the following:

Great rewards are only obtained by great investments. Therefore, as fulfillment is the greatest reward in life, it will require our greatest investment; that is a commitment to excellence.

This shouldn't be difficult to understand. For an example consider 2 men. One man works very hard to provide for himself and his family. Another man doesn't work very hard at all. Rather he steals from others.

At the end of the day both men have equal wealth. The question is – which man is more fulfilled? Is the honest man more fulfilled by his honest labor, or is the thief more fulfilled by his illegal actions?

NO SHORTCUTS

Let's talk about students. When I was in high school, many of my peers were engaged in cheating and getting better grades than they deserved.

It was so bad that I found myself often enticed to cheat too. I mean some of these cheaters were getting straight-A's without working for them and acquiring scholarships they didn't truthfully earn. Why not get in on this seemingly foolproof deal?

"Conscience is a killer," I often tell my children and I know this to be true, for a pure conscience will kill out every thought contrary to your moral compass and thus keep you from following every unrighteous path.

As for me, I felt like I had the biggest conscience of all time. Even though a part of me sometimes wanted to do things which I knew weren't right, my conscience always got in the way. Thank goodness too, for people like me never get away with doing anything wrong. We don't know how to – and even when we do mess up, we're the first ones to tell on ourselves.

The point I'm trying to make is this – even though these cheaters got good grades in high school, I seriously doubt cheating did anything to prepare them for college. Honestly, unless these found some way to cheat through college as well, they were eventually going to have to commit themselves to excellence if they wanted to enjoy the true reward of making good grades.

Maybe they didn't. Maybe they found a way to cheat through college as well. The question is – when will the cheating stop?

The truth is I don't have a clear-cut answer to this question. But I do know that cheating, lying, and the like will always catch up to you – and when they do, it will not be pretty; especially when your time on these regressive paths is defined by an extended stay.

See my mentors taught me many valuable lessons. One of them reveals you can fool some of the people some of the time, but you can never fool all of the people all of the time. As this is surely the case, why try to fool anyone at any time? As it is for certain you will never succeed in this manner, the only person you're really fooling is yourself.

Another lesson reveals that cheaters, liars, and the like will eventually find themselves at the back of the line because there are no shortcuts in life – and as I said before, we will all reap what we sow.

So if you're a cheater, you will be cheated. If you're a liar, you will be both lied on and lied to. Therefore, I call you to always remember the Golden Rule. Do unto others as you would have them do unto you.

DISCOVER YOUR STRENGTHS

Have you ever built anything with your hands? I have, and let me tell you – it is an awesome experience; specifically because of the feeling of achievement you feel afterwards.

Now I also thoroughly appreciated the time I spent working on the project. Here's why – true fulfillment is the end result of honest labor and is not realized only at the conclusion of the initiative. It is realized during the entire process.

Sadly many don't realize this because they aren't working towards their strengths. Trust me; I wouldn't experience too much fulfillment trying to build a car because engineering is not my strong suit. I'm a computer scientist and a very technical one at that. Accordingly, I'll have more success and fulfillment building a computer, a database, or a website because these initiatives are aligned with my strengths and will better position me to excel.

This speaks to one of the more optimal ways of teaching men and women the value and importance of excellence; namely, we have to work with them to discover their strengths and give them opportunities to exercise these particular skills sets (an exercise which I typically execute as I work with groups in the order of determining their life purposes).

THE TURN OF EMPTY LABOR

Next we have to work to make sure these individuals understand the value of their core education and how it relates to and prepares them for fulfilling their life purposes. I know this works because I've seen it work in my life and in the lives of many young persons who I've been blessed to work with. Like me, these remarkable young people understand they must work hard to get to where they want to be in life. Nevertheless, they're not interested in empty labor and neither am I.

What do I mean when I say *empty labor*? With regards to our model of fulfillment, empty labor represents all the paths and activities which aren't moving us forward. Quite the contrary; empty labor always causes us to move backwards while increasing our levels of disappointment and regret.

Accordingly, empty labor is more than a waste of time. It's also a waste of energy and other personal resources, all of which are limited. Consequently, an important facet of living a life of purpose is avoiding the unfulfilling paths of empty labor.

Believe it or not most people get this. The problem usually lies in their levels of commitment to excellence on any terms. Unfortunately some will not commit themselves to excellence unless there is some awesome tangible reward involved; eliminating any expected constancy in their commitment.

As for me and many who I have mentored, we don't require any awesome or tangible rewards to be committed to doing our best. As living a life of purpose is essentially a lifestyle, excellence for us will never be a commodity for barter or a bargaining chip. Excellence is what we strive for everyday because we are continually motivated by the peerless experience of fulfillment.

Notwithstanding, a huge part of excellence is channeling our efforts towards progressive initiatives. Therefore, as there are many endeavors in this life void of fulfillment, it is imperative for us to validate all of our enterprises are worth our investment of excellence. Then and only then will our labor neither be empty nor in vain.

YOU HAVE TO ASK WHY

This is going to be a major part of your reality for a good portion of your life if you have children. I know because of the most popular question my children ask me. That would be – *why?*

Classically my response to this question is almost always *why not* – and if my children don't press the issue, then to me it's not an issue. They straightaway do what they were asked as I sit back in my soft chair comfortably and say to myself, "My, Mr. Anderson; what lovely, obedient children you have…"

However, if they continue to ask *why*, then I know I'm in for at least a 15-minute discussion. So I stop doing whatever I'm doing, put the kettle on, and take a deep breath. 5 minutes later my tea is ready. So we sit down at the kitchen table to discuss the most popular question of all time – why.

Now at this moment I realize a crucial matter; that is I am on trial, for my children are putting me on the hot seat to explain to them (within reason) why they are being asked to do something (usually out of the ordinary) – and because they are all honest and respectful (and because I am not insecure about my authority within my home), this scene is almost always productive. So I usually allow it to play itself out.

As for me, my job is to simply explain to my children (again within reason) the grounds for my request and the value of their compliance; for if I can't even accomplish this simple task, then I must ask myself this critical question – why am I asking my child to do something when I can't in good conscience explain to them the reasoning behind my request?

9 times out of 10 I do have a good reason which I am able to convey to my children. However, there are times when they show me my original position lacks substance and may be a derivative of my own reservations or fears. Plainly speaking, my reasoning is empty. So the question I have to ask myself then is this – do I want to subject my children to my empty reasoning, fears, or any other personal deficit?

Not me; specifically because I hate empty labor possibly more than anything I hate in life, and I don't use the word *hate* often or lightly. Reason being, empty labor represents all the things I've wasted in my life, from the actual loss to the adjacent, agonizing event of a missed opportunity. These collectively serve as a constant reminder that I will never know exactly "what could have been" with regards to the numerous courses taken (or forsaken) and decision made (or unmade) in my life.

Painfully the very sound of those 2 words (i.e. empty labor) reminds me of the time I got lost in the country looking for my wife's home amid thousands of miles of country roads, cow farms, and corn fields. Seriously though, I do consider myself to be a progressive person. Therefore, I don't appreciate setbacks and I strongly dislike wasting my time or any of my resources for that matter.

In particular, I don't like spinning my wheels or finding myself going in the wrong direction to eventually discover I've exerted considerable efforts in an initiative that is conclusively without product. I value my time and my efforts too much to waste. You should too.

This is why both the foundation and apex of this message and the entire Life Pinnacles program is purpose, for purpose is what allows us to channel our efforts, our time, and ultimately our excellence in the most effective manner.

What is more, purpose is what allows me, as a father, to convince my children to comply with each objective which will help them make the most efficient transition to adulthood. After all, isn't this the ultimate aim of parenting? Is it not to effectively raise children to eventually become progressive members of society and leaders of functional families?

AVOIDING A MUTINY

True, I could have the attitude that my children will obey me because I'm their father – and ultimately it does come down to that. However, I've seen the effects of families, organizations, and other offices which are managed predominately in this manner (i.e. via the iron fist) and many of them are in large part dysfunctional.

As I mentioned earlier, my preferred leadership style is consensus. Thus even when I have the power to invoke my will, my preference is still to get buy-in from the group. This sets the stage for each individual to better understand where I'm coming from and where I'm going, simply because I've included them in the decision-making process.

Furthermore, consensus allows me to strengthen my relationship with each member by enhancing our individual levels of communication and trust. This sets the stage for my group to more effectively and surely buy into my vision instead of singly succumbing to my authority. This is crucial beyond measures; for when people feel like all they're doing is succumbing to your authority, you're inviting a mutiny.

Alas, I've seen this firsthand; specifically on some of my earlier projects when I was more of an authoritarian *lead* as opposed to a flexible, yet credible *leader* (notice the emphasis on the variation between *lead* and *leader*). Nonetheless, rebellions can be avoided by leaders who have the insight to recognize that authority must be wielded with great wisdom and sensitivity in order to get the most out of their groups.

This is the primary reason why young people and novices hardly ever find themselves in leadership positions. It's because they lack the wisdom to effectively manage the immense implications and layers of power leaders are often assigned. They also fail to realize a crucial matter which I will offer as another interest point.

> **Being a leader is not about you. It's about the people who are following you.**

Leaders who understand and accept this truth will always be successful in their offices, for they will routinely upgrade their practice to best serve its members simply because they realize the crucial order of importance. For this cause, their rule will be highlighted by persuasion as opposed to the ineffective utilization of the coveted yet hollow iron fist.

On the other hand, leaders who fail to embrace this principle will fatally elevate their desires and perspectives above the group's. This will set off a chain reaction in which the most valuable members of the group leave 1-by-1 until all that remains is a shallow pool of yes-men and yes-women who don't mind capitulating to the single authority of 1 defective leader; even when their single authority is not what's best for the group.

Then again, just because some members do hold-over does not mean they're really invested in this group. Often times they're just hanging around until something better comes along, for the fact that they remained does not mean they are persuaded in the leader's vision or authority.

Therefore, if you as a leader can not sell your followers on your vision by persuasion as opposed to sheer authority, they're not going to be all-in for the following cause – the majority of mankind resists authority, and there is a rebel deep inside even the most peaceful among us.

THE SUMMATION

At the highest level, sound work ethic is effectively fulfilling each role associated with our life offices. This requires each of us to achieve balance, for balance allows us to establish our priorities and dedicate a healthy amount of time in all the initiatives associated with our life purposes.

This speaks to the greatest threat associated with achieving sound work ethic; that is dedicating too much time in one or more of our life offices. Regrettably such actions will cause us to fail in the life offices which are effectively paying the price for our lack of balance. Therefore, we must resist the temptation to follow after the temporary benefits associated with this unfulfilling path.

Furthermore, we must resist the downfall of laziness as this is just as dangerous as falling into the model of a workaholic. Truly, if we want to obtain great prizes in life, we are going to have to make great investments – and each of these will be delineated by a certain measure of personal excellence; particularly in those areas which correspond to our strengths.

So make sure you are playing to your strengths, for these always have some correlation with your purpose.

Finally you must realize a crucial fact of life; namely our lives are segmented into various times and seasons. Each of these will determine how much time we should dedicate to our varying life offices due to the weight of their priorities. This brings me to my final word on work ethic.

Sound work ethic is all about effectively channeling your energies towards your prioritized purposes while being sensitive to your times and seasons. Remember this and your labor will never be without fruit.

CHAPTER 10

Focus

*

"The author taught this living creed — the human mind is as a seed, Which blossomed not from all the weeds, which taint desires and our needs."

AMID THE SUPER-HIGHWAY OF LIFE

One of my mentors was my Uncle Hosea. Uncle Hosea taught me some of my greatest lessons. One in particular was about focus.

"Anderson," he said to me one Sunday afternoon, "remember this one thing."

"Yes Sir," I replied.

He then gave me a stern look and declared, "The only person who knows how to drive on the highway is you."

At first I thought he was making a jest about bad drivers. Then I realized he was going deeper than that. Older folks often do. They make simple comments which have immense meaning and fortune. The question is – can we younger folk catch the deep meanings behind some of their most simple sayings?

I did, at least on that occasion. See what he said had nothing to do with all the poor drivers on the road. On the rather, it had everything to do with me and how I was going to coexist with them for a sure cause – poor drivers are everywhere. From the speed demon, to the woman doing her makeup, to the teenager who is texting, our roads are filled with a surplus of distracted drivers.

The same goes for your quest for fulfillment. The path which leads to your destiny is like a super-highway filled with countless travelers who (like you) are trying to find their purpose.

The problem is many of these travelers are consistently distracted. Consequently, they are swerving out of their lanes, increasing traffic, and making life complicated for those of us who have a steady hand and are abiding by all the rules. The question is – how are you going to deal with them?

Here's the answer – you are going to succeed where they are failing because you are not going to become distracted. You my friend are going to remain focused. Amid the super-highway of life and all the peril, distractions, and wrecks it carries, you are not going to lose sight of any of your life purposes. Let me show you how.

DISTRACTIONS WITHOUT, DISTRACTIONS WITHIN

I don't have any statistics, but I would conjecture nearly 8 out of every 10 wrecks are a result of some human error which can be directly attributed to a lack of focus. Fortunately I have never been in a car accident as a passenger or driver. Yet I am very aware that many have and some have lost their lives. Thus clearly there is a high price involved (specifically when it comes to driving) when we lose our focus, for we are compromising the lives of everyone on the road (including ourselves and those who may be in our vehicle).

Definitively the same should be said for our quest for fulfillment. Although the high price is not nearly as drastic as death, our lack of focus is not only going to negatively affect us. It's also going to have a negative impact on everyone whose destiny is somehow tied to ours.

Here again, this is where I found myself almost 10 years ago when I became a director in IT. See I not only lacked sound work ethic; I also lacked focus. The consequence – a whole world of people were adversely affected, from my wife and children to various social outlets.

Now although I did eventually regain my focus, the truth is I lost it from time to time afterwards. This speaks to the immense challenge associated with remaining focused, for not only do you have to make sure you are not distracted by all the diversions which are not on your path to fulfillment. You have to also make sure you are not distracted by all the diversions which are. This brings us to a relative paradox associated with living a life of purpose which I will offer as an interest point.

> **As we get closer to fulfilling our destiny, we will discover that our greatest challenges are not distractions outside of our life offices. Rather they are distractions within.**

This is why focus is such a critical level; specifically because the distractions within our life offices are often more difficult to detect. However, if you have effectively prioritized your life purposes and have a fundamental awareness of your times and seasons, all you have to do is stay balanced. Only then will you keep these distractions from besetting any of your causes.

THE PROGRESSION PRINCIPLE

Have you heard the fable about the tortoise and the hare? Admittedly this is one of my favorite stories of all time because there are so many lessons to be learned from it.

From now I would like to discuss the real reason why the hare lost the race. Contrary to popular beliefs, it's not necessarily because he was overconfident. Neither is it because the tortoise was faster than we all realized. Quite simply, the hare lost the race because he lost focus.

Now we know this because in the beginning the hare had no intentions of taking a nap during the race. See he was determined to win, for it was his destiny to win. Nature had selectively made him much faster than the tortoise. All he had to do was remain focused on the goal and he was destined to win the race.

However, at some point during the race, his extreme levels of overconfidence caused him to lose focus. This loss subjected him to poor judgment and eventually caused him to take an untimely, unplanned siesta at a critical juncture in the race. Thus we conclude the hare lost the race the moment he lost focus, and once again we find the overconfident falling quarry to underachievement.

Noticeably this fable lends itself to a crucial aspect regarding the Pinnacle of Purpose; that is, if we're not progressively moving forward on our path to fulfillment, we will experience relapse with regards to the milestones and levels we have already crossed.

We see this clearly by analyzing how the hare's lack of focus (which is the fifth level of the Pinnacle of Purpose) triggered both poor judgment and poor work ethic (which are the third and fourth levels of the Pinnacle of Purpose). Appropriately I refer to this example as the *"Progression Principle."* It reveals the following:

If we are not consistently progressing on our path to fulfillment, we will find ourselves regressing in every aspect of our lives.

Here's what it all comes down to – we're not going to grow if we're not doing those things which foster growth. Instead we're going to experience some measure of decline and will continue in decline until we learn how to stay focused.

I DID THIS TO MYSELF

One way in which I lost focus in those days was concerning my health. I surmise many of us have a similar story so I will share mine.

I was in my mid 20's when I was diagnosed with pretty severe cases of high blood pressure and high cholesterol – and no wonder. Even though I got in the occasional basketball game and had spent most of my youth as an athlete, I had lost focus on my health. It was one of many things which suffered as a result of my overzealous, ill-planned drive for success in those days.

It was also a result of my ignorance. I mean I was in the gym lifting weights or playing basketball almost 5 times a week. Anyone who saw me would think I was in the 95th percentile for healthy young adults.

Quite frankly I felt that way too. On the exterior I appeared to be in the best shape of my life. Yet beneath the surface my health was deteriorating and for reasons well within my range of control.

Now there were various warning signs along this regressive road I was traveling. For one, my body would regularly speak to me, from the occasional shortness of breath to chronic stomach pains. Yet regardless of all these warning signs, I wasn't compelled to take any serious actions.

Then one day my declining health put me in a hospital and in the most excruciating pain I had ever been in. It was exactly then that I realized I had gone too far in disregarding my health. I had to make some changes fast or this was only going to get worse.

So I went home with various pamphlets and papers which provided me with information related to reclaiming my health. Ironically they were the same papers I had received during health seminars at work, from my local gym, and from my family doctor; the same papers I had ignored and crammed towards the bottom of my nightstand. Remorsefully, when I compared the papers to each other and saw how similar they were, all I could do was shake my head and confess, "I did this to myself."

ALL YOU HAVE IS YOUR HEALTH

It goes without saying that one of your most crucial possessions in life is your health, for it is impossible to have a progressive life if you're consistently in poor health. Hence the axiom is true. All you really have is your health. For this cause, the foundation of each or your life offices is centered on your ability to keep yourself in good health (i.e. physical, spiritual, and emotional).

If you don't believe me, consider all of your life offices and ask yourself this question – would I be able to fulfill my role in this office if I didn't have the compulsory physical, spiritual, or emotional stamina?

I believe all of our answers will be similar and in the negative. Hence we can make the following conclusion – if we are not healthy in every area of our lives, the areas where we are unhealthy will eventually have a negative impact on our life offices.

Of course you can try to conceal the unhealthy aspects of your life or ignore all the potential consequences they could have. Yet in the end it's going to come out – and when it does, you're not the only one who is going to suffer. If you have a family, they're going to have to do more to account for your immobility.

In the best case this setback may be temporary. Thus you'll be able to manage the interim period of immobility and soon return to normalcy. Hopefully you will have learned your lesson in the process.

However, in the worst cases this immobility may be either long-term or permanent. Now your loved ones are being asked to change their lives drastically to account for your failure to take every facet of your health seriously. Therefore, as the quality of your life (and the lives of those around you) is indeed dependent upon your health, healthy living should be a top priority in your quest for fulfillment.

FOR EVERY ACTION THERE IS A REACTION

Unfortunately I have witnessed the inevitable conclusion of unhealthy living on several occasions; more often than I would have liked. Sometimes the family pulls together and endures the drastically difficult changes in their lives due to one member's lack of focus. Other times the family is torn apart. The negative impact is too great for one or more members to endure and perhaps justifiably so.

All things considered, I would encourage everyone to be willing to sacrifice and to bear each other's burdens. True, it'd be different if the circumstance of poor health was not self-inflicted. In these occasions, there would be no excuse for a family member to turn their back on another simply because love is not selfish – and deserting someone who becomes ill for no fault of their own is a purely selfish act.

Nonetheless, the focal person in this example is not any of those persons affected by the adverse situation; rather it is the individual who becomes ill. Accordingly, every reaction by those innocent external parties must be initially gauged by the reason why their loved one came to be in such difficult straits.

Seeing as we've already evaluated this situation when the focal person becomes ill without fault, we should now analyze those situations when the focal person willfully enters into a poor state of health because of a lack of focus.

First of all, it is impossible to determine how those affected are going to react in these cases. What we can determine is this – their reaction will always be to some degree justifiable due to the defensible nature of cause and effect. Plainly speaking, don't be surprised if someone hits you if you hit them first. If they don't then all's well. It's your lucky day.

However, if they do hit you back, you do not have a legitimate reason to be taken aback; for even the Good Book originally promotes the "eye for an eye" and "tooth for a tooth" philosophies. So don't be shocked if your consistent, regressive actions don't result in progressive reactions. This is hardly how things go down.

Nevertheless, and although it is a certain folly, many are yet determined to somehow get even in occasions which are visibly unfair. What these fail to realize is a simple life lesson which reveals the following – for every action there is an equal and opposite reaction, and you have no control over the reaction. So take my advice and be very thoughtful of all your actions – and do not be distracted, for actions following distractions generally lead to adverse reactions. Moreover, distractions are some of the deadliest obstructions you will find on your path to fulfillment. This brings us to another interest point.

> **Distractions are as slippery slopes, for it becomes increasingly more difficult to regain your focus once you begin to lose it.**

This is precisely why distractions are so lethal. Their slippery nature makes them near-to-impossible to escape once the slide has been instigated; let alone the fact that you are hopeless to the subsequent aftermath of each like episode.

Finally, as these are all certain truths borne out by countless witnesses, do not fail to heed the warning signs; precisely when you first begin to stray and realize you are getting off course. Otherwise you will be as many who came this far in their quest only to revert back to a life of disappointment and regret – and rapidly; for the moment you become distracted, you begin traveling backwards and much faster than you realize.

THE BEST OF A TROUBLED WORLD

Fortunately I was able to travel the lesser of two evil roads in my personal quest for fulfillment; for although I was forced to learn my lesson on focus the hard way, I did not incur any permanent or short-term losses. Providentially the majority of the suffering per my lack of focus was on my part and rightfully so.

This speaks to the great opportunities which exist and remain for each of us even after we have committed both tragic and not-so-tragic errors. See not only can we recover; we can also learn valuable lessons from these difficult experiences.

I like to think of these situations as "the best of a troubled world." Here's the key – we must learn from the experience and keep ourselves from repeating the same mistakes. This is important for a patented reason which I will offer as another interest point.

> **As we travel the path to fulfillment, we will be forced to repeat all of our failed tests until we pass them.**

Truly this is one of the greatest lessons I could offer you in this composition. It is also one of few lessons I find myself conveying to those in my life offices on almost a weekly basis; for when I finally came to this realization, I not only recovered from my former life of excess distractions. I became what you might call a "master of focus."

CHANNELING YOUR ENERGY TOWARDS YOUR DESTINY

My evidence is simply the year 2012. In 2012 I was serving as a program manager (this was prior to launching Life Pinnacles but during the time in which I was formulating the program).

Now at the height of this position, I was managing 2 programs and 12 projects between them. This may not sound like much on paper; but if you have an IT background, then you already know how less than 1% of all program or project managers are even capable of managing 12 projects simultaneously — and even for this select few, it's a certain high-risk proposition.

As for me, I'm not so sure I was in this elite 1%. All I know is that the economy was having a negative impact on business. This prompted management to lay off several contractors and employees.

At the same time, the workload did not decrease; neither did it stay the same. Much to the chagrin of those of us who remained, our workload sky-rocketed.

I'll never forget the feeling I had once the news came to me. I had already seen my workload increase in recent months and was struggling to manage 8 projects. How was I going to be able to effectively manage 12 with a smaller project team?

Before discussing how I would be able to manage 12, let's first talk about how I was managing 8. Beyond the obvious, crucial factor of balance, I also kept a schedule – but not just any schedule. This particular schedule was an Excel spreadsheet which captured all my daily activities to the very hour. Accordingly, by following this detailed schedule, I found myself spending my time more efficiently than any other season in my life.

This is precisely why I was able to effectively manage 8 projects. Nevertheless, once I got to 12 projects, I came to the realization that there were no hours left in my day to concede to my professional office without compromising the others. My schedule had reached critical mass. So I took a deep breath, got my thoughts together, and took it up with my manager. Surely he would understand, wouldn't he?

The truth is I can't say he did; neither can I say he didn't. What I can tell you is this – due to budget constraints, he informed me that I was not going to be getting any help any time soon. No sir; I was expected to manage these 12 projects with a skeleton crew with similar success as I had managed 8 with a full team.

To this day I refer to that chapter in my life as my "Rapunzel Experience." Like Rapunzel, I was being asked to turn straw into gold – her literally, me figuratively.

Further symbolically, I was staring down a similar path I had travelled almost 7 years before. This vantage point made my eventual decision very straightforward, for I had already confirmed that this particular path was in the long run unfulfilling – and I could feel myself losing focus due to the corresponding decrease in my levels of balance.

So there I was, somewhere fixed between a rock and a hard place. Consequently (and as the saying goes), something had to give. Either I was going to follow a path which I knew was broken, or I was going to stay focused on what was most important.

Now to me the answer was simple. I had already seen the damage a lack of focus can cause and had fortunately survived it with my family still intact. The last thing I wanted to do was walk down a path I had already confirmed would negatively impact the people in the world who I loved the most.

All the same, the economy was struggling in those days while the financial forecast on the whole was very grim. For that reason, I could not find a single shred of support for the difficult decision I was preparing to make outside of my own personal resolve and convictions.

Perhaps you feel that I was in a "lose-lose" scenario; for remaining in my professional office would cause me to regress with regards to my quest for fulfillment, while resigning would almost certainly compromise my ability to provide for my family long-term.

The truth is that these were my initial sentiments too; that is until I considered this situation faithfully and honestly. That's when I realized that I was not in a "lose-lose" scenario at all. I was in a "win-lose" scenario, for my decision to resign would cause me to *win* with regards to my quest for fulfillment – and although this may not have been the way I viewed the situation at the first, it was the most accurate view to be seen; hence the unlimited value in thinking things through.

Now this matter lends itself to perhaps the most confounded aspect of this account; that is the fact that staying in this position would be a loss in spite of the tangible benefits involved. However, this reality is not so baffling if you consider all the areas in which my life would suffer if I remained in this impossible position – and this ultimately made my decision, for the sum of these losses was infinitely greater than all the physical benefits this position could offer me.

Then again, my mind went back to a crucial life lesson which I offered as an interest point in the prior section; that is, we will revisit all of our failed tests in our pursuit of fulfillment until we succeed them. Subsequently, I realized I was being tested to see whether or not I would venture down the same path I had taken years prior.

It was exactly then that I witnessed the awesome power of focus – and with great conviction I resigned from that position. Then I renewed my focus and channeled it towards my destiny. Decisively these actions led me to begin creating the framework of Life Pinnacles.

Ultimately this is the high-level purpose of focus. It is to prepare you to walk the final miles on your path to fulfillment by channeling all your energies toward your destiny no matter how unpopular it might be or how unwise it may appear to others.

Furthermore, this is where my spiritual life played an invaluable role in my ability to make the progressive choice. Amazingly, during the entire development I had a sense of confirmation growing inside of me that this was my time. In spite of the flailing economy and all the other reasons why stepping out on faith was not a good idea on paper, my spiritual life had already prepared me to do so. So I did, and the rest is history.

THE SUMMATION

Focus is one of the most critical levels of the Pinnacle of Purpose because it allows us to effectively channel our spiritual and physical energies. This is important because there are excess distractions along the path to fulfillment. Some of these are external to us. Some of them are internal. Ultimately we have to be cautious of all of them; especially the distractions within.

In doing so, we will be able to guard one of our most important possessions – our health. Needless to say, to endure the physical and emotional grind associated with our quest, we must consistently be in good health. Otherwise we will lack the several energies required to achieve our goals.

Additionally you must be committed to making continued progress on your path as this is the validation of your focus. With awesome levels of single-mindedness, you must have your eyes on the immediate objective at all times as you make your way towards achievement. In any other model you are fatefully moving backwards or in some direction other than your destiny.

This is true because none of us remain the same from day to day. We are always changing, often unknowingly. Therefore, whether by default or by choice, every one of us is moving towards some direction or goal.

This is precisely why we must always be focused. Else we may wake up one morning confounded as to our station in life, for we have no idea where we are at or how we got there.

Lastly I would offer a warning – your destiny, should you not take it by force, can be acquired and thus enjoyed by someone other than you. Don't let this happen. Don't fall into a "de-facto" destiny. Do whatever it takes to stay focused and hold onto what is yours. This brings me to my final word on focus.

The only way to get where we are going in life is to stay focused on the path. Otherwise we will surely be distracted and there's no telling how damaging the distraction will be or where it will lead.

CHAPTER 11

Patience

*

"The wise of men shall learn to wait, and loathe
the things that he should hate; Resisting cries to
deviate, he's never too early, and never too late."

HOW LONG ARE YOU WILLING TO WAIT FOR IT?

The sixth level of the Pinnacle of Purpose is patience. Clearly this is a natural development; for after we achieve the highest level of focus, we will have to patiently wait for an opportunity to enter into an office in which we can fulfill our purpose.

Strategically this opportunity will not appear until we've proven ourselves and our mastery of all the levels we've already traversed. Less we find ourselves walking into an office prematurely and not positioned to succeed.

This reality proves our life purposes are not fulfilled overnight. They, like all worthwhile endeavors, take time – and we will never know at the outset just how long it's going to take.

Now if you're like me, you don't know too many people who are patient by nature. I myself, prior to following my own path to fulfillment, was potentially the most impatient person of all time. Thus very needless to say, patience was the most difficult level for me to master — and this will likely be the case for many who read this book. As a result of our human nature and the rapid pace at which our world is moving, patience is going to present many challenges for each of us.

Before discussing these, I would like to offer my vote of confidence on this matter by stating that anyone can achieve patience simply because I have. Then again, one of my preferred sayings reveals the following — he who can have patience, can have what he will. That is to say, you can have anything in life if you're willing to wait for it. Hence the question of the hour regarding your destiny is simply this — how long are you willing to wait for it?

WHEN YOUR WAY ISN'T BEST

Now the first opportunity for us to increase our patience is usually as small children; expressly if we have parents who understand its immense value. If yours did, then they probably worked tirelessly to get you to appreciate the time it takes to get where you're going and to acquire what you want. Even if yours didn't, life has a natural way of teaching us patience in spite of how vehemently we often resist it.

As for me, I had a crash course with patience as a very young man. In the course of 1 year I became a husband and a father, the 2 life offices which have required the greatest measures of patience from me as a man. I'll start this discussion by addressing my transition from a young bachelor to a young husband.

Like many young men, the 3 words which best described me on my wedding day were excited, nervous, and unprepared. In hindsight (which is of course 20-20), my greatest lack of appreciation was towards my unpreparedness. Unlike many young couples, my wife and I didn't go through any premarital counseling. Sure we had the occasional one-off conversation with aunts, uncles, and fictive kin, but nothing formal or dedicated.

Honestly this is one of my greatest regrets as a husband. Now that I am older and much, much wiser, I believe every young couple should go through dedicated premarital counseling with specific objectives.

If you consider the divorce rate in our country, you could hardly disagree. The fact of the matter is many young men and women are entering into one of the most challenging life offices unprepared and without dedicated support. How successful do you think they are going to be?

As for my case, the focal question is – why didn't I go through any premarital counseling? After all, my wife's father was more than willing to set up sessions for us to speak with ministers at his church about the huge decision we were preparing to make.

Besides this it was free. Yet regardless of these facts, I declined any formal premarital counseling for a seriously stupid reason – I thought I knew (at that early juncture) pretty much everything I needed to know to have a successful marriage.

Do you remember my earlier appraisal about the overconfident? If not let me remind you – the overconfident will always underachieve. Accordingly, because I was foolishly overconfident in my extremely limited ability on this wise, I had foolishly decreased my prospects of achieving in my role as a husband.

Now the reality that I was completely ignorant to the fact that I was overconfident is inconsequential. My ignorance set me up and eventually caused me to underachieve in one of the most important life offices I would ever hold – and although I would eventually recover from this crucial error in judgment, the fact remains that I suffered various setbacks in my marriage simply because I was too set in my own ways.

This reality and the negative consequences I met because of it have taught me one of the greatest lessons I have learned in life. The lesson – more often than not, our way is not the best way. The only way we will realize it is if we follow the guidelines of patience, all of which allow us to effectively listen to others and genuinely consider their points of view.

THE IMPORTANCE OF TIME MANAGEMENT

Along these lines, patience is a key factor in our ability to accept good advice. This can be proven by the inverse; namely, the primary reason why many fail to take good advice is because they do not want to adjust their schedule. This is because adjusting our schedule forces us to put off those things we had already planned to do. Consequently, every instance in which we adjust our schedule is highlighted by some interval in which we are forced to wait.

Although this may not be obvious at first glance, I assure each reader it is true. Take me for example. Like the popular majority, I maintained a long list of things I wanted to get done. However, I only had a limited amount of time to accomplish each initiative.

So what did I do? Did I update my list to differentiate between those things which I had time to do and those things which I did not? You bet I didn't. No, I was intent on finding a way to somehow cram all these activities into a window of time incapable of effectively supporting each. Like many before me and many who are following after, I had been deceived into taking the illusory shortcuts in my life – and 1 too many, for even 1 shortcut taken in life is 1 too much.

As we have prior stated, there are numerous troubles associated with taking shortcuts in life. With specific regards to patience, the primary trouble is this – each shortcut taken reinforces one of the most critical deficits of our quest for fulfillment; that is the inability of many to effectively manage their time towards their fulfillment.

For this cause, time management is indeed one of the most important aspects of living a life of purpose. It begins with the understanding that your destiny is not personified by you necessarily getting to do everything you want to do; rather it is illustrated by you doing everything you were designed to do.

Here lies inflexion. Explicitly, when we first embark on our quest for fulfillment, we are not fully aware of all the things we were designed to do. For that reason, many of our original desires and plans are not perfectly related to our destiny. This is why time management is so crucial, for it allows us to effectively determine how we should best spend our time in the order of fulfilling our destiny.

This also speaks to the immense power of patience, for patience is the critical link which allows us to manage our time effectively. Here's how – patience strategically eliminates the occasions in our lives which are not on our critical path of fulfillment by forcing us to discontinue many irrelevant activities; all of which are slowing us down and increasing the difficulty of our quest.

Purposefully, this exercise makes the difficult task of adjusting your schedule as simple as it is necessary. Thus we conclude that one of the primary objectives of patience is to cause us to dedicate our time to the initiatives which will keep us on our path to fulfillment and the consequent concession of those initiatives which won't – and this is the foundation of time management.

THINK TWICE AND GET ADVICE

Very needless to say, I wish I knew all of this and more prior to my engagement; yet I didn't. Neither can I go back in time to rewrite history. All I can do is honestly share my mistakes and recoveries with others such that they too may recover or avoid these errors in judgment altogether. This is a focal pillar of progressive living which I encourage all to live by.

All things considered, the first year of my marriage was awesome in spite of my self-crippling. The only truly distressing time I can remember was when my wife gave birth to our first child. Although we joke about it now, the experience wasn't funny at the time; not at all.

Without going into the details, I would simply state that I was not wholly prepared for the totality of the delivery room experience. Consequently, it didn't go as I had originally hoped or planned; far from it actually.

See I thought the whole thing would be a piece of cake. I would be there for my wife through the whole ordeal as cool as a cucumber. Having a baby was no big deal. It was just another challenge in life that my wife and I were going to get through together.

If you're laughing now then I don't blame you; specifically because you already perceive how ill-fated this event would play itself out. Unfortunately I did not at the time, for it was sheer ignorance for me to assume having a baby was not a "big deal" simply because I wasn't the one delivering the baby – she was. I wasn't going to be the one in excruciating pain; that would be Mrs. Anderson.

Perhaps I didn't consider this proposition thoroughly before the delivery started; but let me tell you, I heard it loud and clear once the fateful process began. After which I said to myself, "I'll not be back here again."

Still (and like I said before), my wife and I both joke about that extraordinary adventure to this day simply because it is important for us not to take ourselves too seriously. As I often tell my children – if you can't laugh at yourself, then you're setting yourself up to incur both hurt and hard feelings. Moreover, if you can't laugh at yourself, you don't have a legitimate right to laugh at anyone else.

As for the moral of this story (which I purposely never completely divulged), it is a reinforcement of the need for everyone to have input and direction in life. Trust me; no one who does anything for the first time should ever place too much confidence in their potential of success.

This is especially true if they're not open to receiving ample guidance. So take my advice and in every life situation be committed to thinking at least twice. Additionally, seek out wise men and women for their advice (especially if you're thinking about being in the delivery room when your wife gives birth).

LEADING FROM BEHIND

So I escaped my delivery room debacle with both my life and marriage intact. Things were finally going to get back to normal, right? Wrong! We just had a baby remember? My beautiful young wife was now a beautiful young mother. Is there a difference? You bet there's a difference.

A time or 2 I've been called an educated fool. Sadly I'd have to concede to this undesirable moniker because that's exactly what I've been. Alas, even though my wife had become a mother, I wanted and foolishly expected her to continue to be the person she was when she was singly my wife.

My reasons for this non-sensible perspective are as inconsequential as they are unjustifiable. After all, it was our joint decision to have a child. The problem was I never considered what having a child would mean and how it would affect what I believed was a pretty awesome marriage; hence the limitless value of thinking twice and being open to sound counsel.

All things considered, it was too late now. The genie was out of the bottle. The cat was out of the bag. Our reservations for 2 had evolved into a dinner party for 3, and growing. Alas, things were never going to be the same.

Now the greatest change was in the fact that I was no longer #1 on my wife's list – our child was. Subsequently our household developed the metaphoric *family line*, a figurative line which specifies the order of who gets taken care of first, second, third, and so on in the family.

For 10 short months I was at the front of the line. Yet as destiny would have it, I've been at the back of the line ever since – and although I didn't see it then, the back of the line is exactly where I belonged.

Gentlemen, it's where we all belong. Whether we realize or not, if we are going to be the leaders of progressive, functional family units, we're going to have to learn to put everyone else in our families first. We're going to have to learn how to lead from behind.

GET YOURSELF OUT OF THE WAY

People hear me make statements like this today and they get very excited; especially women. More recently my wife has often heard other women tell her she is fortunate to be married to "a guy like me." That's when we both laugh, although she tends to laugh harder and longer. Then, fretfully, an awkwardly sheepish look comes upon my face as I kindly plead, "Honey, please stop laughing…"

So why do you think she laughs? Clearly it's because I didn't become a pronounced husband by any standard or an effective leader overnight.

Unfortunately it took several difficult years and moments when neither I nor my wife knew just how this marriage was going to play itself out.

Without going into the details of those years, I want to discuss how I was transformed from an average to a progressive husband starting with this realism – the leader of any functional entity must be the greatest servant in the group.

In many veins this model is referred to as servant leadership, an highly effective leadership style which enhances a group by the proficient service of its leaders. The result – everyone in the group is edified and positioned to reach their maximum potential.

Observably the concept of servant leadership is not difficult to understand. Neither is it hard to implement. My problem then was my preconceived notions about what it meant to "be the man."

Granted I wasn't as bad off as some men I knew. The truth is I was considerably farther along. Still, and as I said earlier, there is little to no value in comparing yourself to anyone else; specifically when the person you are comparing yourself to is not even on your level. All this does is cause you to feel better about yourself than you should (and to your hurt I might add).

In my case, I wasn't a victim of unproductive comparisons. I was just flat out stubborn – and because I thought I was "the man," I was under the false impression that my wife would and should listen to me for that reason alone. This made it very difficult for me to ever truly appreciate or consider her point of view, a clear detriment to the model of servant leadership.

So what happened? Well for many months, even years, we were in a continual power struggle over the evolution of our family to the point that our family failed to progressively evolve.

Now we weren't necessarily trying to go in 2 completely different directions. We wouldn't have lasted if we were. The problem was in the details (i.e. the "fine print" of our individual vision for the family). Visibly these were manifested in every occasion in which we were initially unwilling to compromise.

Here lies the greatest source of conflict in every marriage; that is failing to consider how a successful marriage is based upon your ability to accept the "details" of your significant other. This is a critical error for a sure cause which I will offer as another interest point.

> **The purpose of marriage is not to change your spouse into the person you want them to be. Rather it is to help facilitate the process in which your spouse evolves into the person they were destined to be.**

Decisively this knowledge helped revolutionize my understanding of what it meant to be "the man" while also revealing to me the greatest source of my failures as a husband. Explicitly, I was unknowingly trying to make my wife become someone she wasn't because I was more focused on what I wanted *from her* as opposed to what I wanted *for her*. Trust me; there's a huge difference.

So what did I do? Well I was still intent on being the man and rightfully so. However, I needed to redefine what being the man meant by discovering all those things which it entailed. All I had to do was get myself out of the way and the path became luminously clear.

THE BREEZE OF COMPROMISE

Naturally my call to servant leadership led me to a door with the following inscription – *COMPROMISE*! Although it is often regarded as a sign of weakness, compromise is paradoxically a sign of our truest strength; for the most difficult paths to tread in life are those which go against our nature.

As far as nature goes, all of us (men and women alike) are largely committed to getting what we want and doing things our way. This is why it takes strong men and women to compromise, for we are effectively relinquishing our desire to get what we want by taking this path. Like a fish swimming upstream, we are going against the grain.

Classically this model speaks to why so many people don't like to compromise. It is also why so many families are dysfunctional, for not only is reaching a compromise a difficult enterprise within and of itself; the inevitable aftermath is that someone (often everyone) is going to lose out.

Nevertheless, here's the reality you should be considering – if you're not regularly compromising with your significant others, you are already in some manner losing out. The question is – how do you want to lose? That is to ask, do you want to follow a path where you are guaranteed to gain to account for your loss? Or would you prefer to follow a path where your loss is compounded and without any upshot or increase?

Personally I have never liked a "lose-lose" situation and try to avoid them at all costs. Therefore, I was more than prepared to try my hand with compromise. As the saying goes – happy wife, happy life.

Now learning to compromise in the beginning wasn't easy, for compromise, as one might expect, is a lifestyle and not a singular event. Consequently, when I committed myself to this path, I was giving myself over to the unpredictable winds of change and there was effectively no turning back. I was in it for the long haul.

Following, I realized just how divided my wife and I had become over the years. I also realized the immense effort it would take to get us on the same page. See although we never considered it, my wife and I were never on the same page; not from the beginning — and as we consistently failed to compromise, we found ourselves growing further and further apart.

As a matter of fact, we had been growing apart from the very start of our marriage. It just took me several years to realize it and the damage it had done to our family.

Yet when I came to this realization, I began strategizing how I could use compromise to finally get us on the same page — and as difficult as it was in the beginning, I felt a gentle breeze growing towards the end. The compromise I had once feared was now becoming my friend.

ARE YOU LISTENING?

Now this matter lends itself to the importance of focus. As husbands and fathers, our focus should not be on getting what we want. Rather our focus should be on making sure everyone in our family has everything they need. This leads us to a focal interest point which reveals one of the greatest responsibilities of all husbands and fathers.

> *To be an effective leader, your primary focus should be attending to the needs of others and ensuring the needs of the many are not comprised by the desires of a few.*

Markedly this realism brings out a focal aspect of manhood; explicitly, being the man does not suggest you are licensed to rule over your family like some drunken king on a power trip. On the contrary, being the man suggests you are able to effectually lead your family in the best direction for the family as a whole.

This speaks to a terrific aspect concerning compromise, a certain make-or-break proposition as it were. Unequivocally, if you are going to have any success at compromise, you must listen carefully and constantly to those you are leading. Else you will be consistently unaware of their needs and thus unable to resolve them.

Honestly a smile comes upon my face as I write this particular line. See of all the things I'm not and have never been, I have become a good listener over the course of my life – and as you would expect, my ability to effectively listen to others is one of my greatest strengths as a husband, a father, and a friend to all those within my life offices.

The question is – why is listening so important when it comes to compromise? I will tell you while addressing my answer specifically to men and in the vein of intimate relations.

Now men, whether or not you realize it, women are profoundly emotional creatures. It's one of many things which makes them so attractive. Yet simultaneously, it also complicates the communication process.

If you can't follow this line of thought, just consider yourself or anyone who becomes emotional for any cause (e.g. death, pain, or any kind of personal loss). What do you notice about them as far as their ability to communicate? Exactly; it's harder for them to communicate effectively.

In this regard, women will often say 3 or 4 things at once; but they are actually trying to make only 1 point. The question for us men then is simple – what in the world are we supposed to do? Here's the sure answer – you listen closely and you do your best to connect the dots.

Now this matter lends itself to one of the various facets of the artistic nature of women in general. Because of their natural reliance and affinity towards their emotions, their communication style is often indirect. As such, their conversations are better depicted by breadcrumbs than a straight line.

This is precisely why we men must learn how to connect the dots. In essence, we must learn how to follow the breadcrumbs our women are leaving for us, for they will often communicate in stories and narratives utilizing similes, metaphors, and other grammatical expressions which most of us men haven't considered since grade school (if we considered them then). Therefore, if you're going to have a fruitful relationship, you're going to have to figure out what they're saying.

No doubt this is a challenge of epic proportion. Yet should you accept this challenge and should you by Jove succeed, you will clearly see the picture your woman is painting. Then you can show her you were listening and keep going.

You can of course do it the hard way, but I would advise against it. Transforming yourself into a good listener may not be an easy enterprise, but I guarantee you it will be well worth it; for every good woman appreciates a man who listens to them and will usually invest more in him.

Moreover, if you fail on this wise, the lovely breeze of compromise you felt earlier in your quest may very well turn into violent storms of confrontation. Trust me; you don't want this. You want to move your family and your marriage forward. So when your woman is talking, remember to do 2 things: connect the dots and make sure you're listening.

EXPRESS YOURSELF

I was sharing this information with some young men recently. What do you suppose their reaction was to my advice?

To be quite honest they didn't have a lot of pushback. After all, my logic was sound and somewhat undeniable. What is more, most of us men aren't as inconsiderate as we're often portrayed to be. The problem is a few ill-equipped men often give the rest of us a bad rep. It's just another manner in which life is unfair.

Nonetheless, the pushback I did receive from my group was sure and I heard them loud and clear. Their biggest complaint (a classic to say the least) was that the women in their lives were *COMPLICATED*. They then went on to tell me all the reasons why they felt this way.

Comically they carried on for so long that I had to stop them so we didn't go too far over our allotted time for this discussion. That's when I dropped a one-word bomb on them, soundly declaring, "*PATIENCE…*"

I'll never forget the look on one young man's face as he repeated the word back to me. "Patience?!" he both asked and exclaimed.

"Yes patience," I replied almost laughing because of the incredulous look on his face.

Several of them then went on to tell me all the ways they felt they were already being patient with their women. So I encouraged them to continue to be patient. However, this set off another round of complaints and pushback.

Now I could have let them keep going, but I didn't. Their kvetching was getting us nowhere fast. So I stopped them again and declared, "It's quite simple actually. You should all go home and leave your women… That's right. Just go on home and kick them out."

Did that get their attention? You bet it did. One guy even looked at the man next to him with a skeptical look on his face and asked, "Is he serious?"

"I'm serious," I said, "I mean if all of these women you are talking about are so bad, why are you with them? You're strapping, colorful young chaps. Surely you can do better."

I then began repeating back to them all the things they were saying to me. This caused for the room to become deathly silent, for it was one thing for them to complain about their women. It was another thing for them to hear it from me.

"You know what I think?" I asked, then continuing, "I think none of your women are as bad as you're making them out to be. The problem is you're not communicating your feelings to them. So you're frustrated and you're voicing your frustrations to me. Am I right?"

One by one they began to nod their heads. A few of the men even looked around the room to make sure everyone else was nodding. I didn't mind this though. I believe solidarity is important among men; especially when the subject of our agreement is progressive. Honesty always is and that was my message to them. They had to be honest with their women.

Now that didn't necessarily mean they needed to become confrontational. It just meant they had to express their feelings for the following cause – if they did not make their women aware of their frustrations, they could never work through them.

Moreover, if they failed in this endeavor, these men had no one to be upset with but themselves; for how could their women "do better" if they didn't know they were potentially doing something wrong?

Here's the conclusion of this episode – in order to resolve their frustrations, these men were going to have to express themselves. So I told them this, much to their chagrin; for as sure as most women are emotional, most men are closed when it comes to their feelings. Thus expressing ourselves as men will usually be to some degrees challenging.

Here again, this is in large part because the true concept of being a man has regrettably been downgraded. All the same, a real man has no issue displaying emotion or expressing himself and his true feelings, for he knows such actions are as healthy as they are true. Therefore, he is open and honest in all of his dealings, his feelings, and his emotions – and as every progressive relationship is built upon communication and trust, real men will constantly step outside of themselves to ensure this foundation is always strong.

Fortunately I was able to convey this message to all the young men in my group. I then closed by letting them in on a sure reality. With one finger raised I cautioned them saying, "Now don't expect your women, as wonderful as they are, to start making any changes right away. Enjoying a progressive marriage or any relationship for that matter is a process, and reaping the benefits of such an awesome experience does not come suddenly. It comes gradually. So be patient with each other and enjoy the ride. Class dismissed…"

A NEVER-ENDING INVESTMENT

Now the primary reason why I was able to make the transformation from impatient to longsuffering is both classic and sure – I had 4 children. Honestly all you need is 1 and you know what I mean. Raising a child requires laser eyesight, catlike reflexes, and (you guessed it) patience.

As for me, all I have to consider are the countless times I've repeated myself in the past 10 years. On this wise, if I had a quarter for every time I told one of my children the same thing more than once, I would have enough money to pay off my house. I may even have enough left over to buy a new car.

As you would expect, constantly repeating myself was frustrating for me when my children were very young. Then I, educated fool that I was, realized this is the way of all children and mine were no different. See children are naturally forgetful in large part because their brains are still developing. Consequently, we parents must be committed to showing our children increasing levels of patience.

Amazingly this wasn't a difficult lesson for me to learn; specifically because I clearly understood the reason why I needed to be patient with my children. Yet I can't say the same for my wife.

In the beginning of our marriage, I found it difficult to be consistently patient with her because I honestly felt she didn't have any justifiable excuses for most of her failures (presumed or actual). After all, she was an adult. Why was she struggling (by my selfish, inaccurate, and often inconsiderate standards) to be the wife and mother I thought she should be?

Now although there was an answer, I was unable to discover it because my ill-voiced frustrations caused her to become overly defensive. Consequently, I became overly belligerent – and thus she became even more defensive until she began to withdraw. Alas, for many unfulfilling years we never saw past the first frame of this disastrous cycle.

As good fortune would have it, I met a man who had the answer I was seeking. From him I learned how to express myself in a manner conducive for resolution by eliminating my frustrations, a crucial step which would allow my love for my wife and all mankind to serve as both the baseline and the aim of all my communications.

It was exactly then that my wife stopped getting defensive; for as my approach had changed for the better, her response changed in like manner – and for the first time in a long time, my wife had a real productive conversation. Decisively, this was the first step in a series of steps which allowed us to finally get on the same page.

The results were astounding; for as my increased patience had increased my ability to listen, I began to see myself for who I was and had been for many years. That is a husband with substantial room for growth in his own right, substantially more room than my wife.

This is a major reason why I felt it was in my best interest to show her even greater measures of patience than I was showing my children; for as I began to truly appreciate her point of view, I came to the realization that I needed her to be even more patient with me.

So before you point your finger at someone else for their lack, stop and point your finger first at yourself. Then consider all the ways in which you are not perfect, for this reflection will usually cause you to drop whatever you were imprudently planning to say.

Even if it doesn't eliminate your need to address the matter, you will at least do so in a more productive manner because you are better aware of your flaws. This awareness should increase your levels of empathy and keep you from (as my grandmother would say) "acting a fool."

Perhaps this is the most critical lesson on patience. The fact of the matter is we all have issues in our lives we need to resolve. So if you are with someone who is committed to working on their issues, then it is incumbent upon you to be patient with them. You must be their biggest supporter and their greatest source of strength, not a dissenting voice which is irrationally tearing them down.

Furthermore, if you're with someone, it's likely because they are worth it. So be willing to invest in them while always remembering the following interest point.

> **The greatest investment you can make in someone you love is your patience, for your patience is tied to your greatest possession in life – your time.**

So there you have it. If you want to have the best marriage or relationship this life can afford you, increase the worth of your loved ones by giving them your never-ending investment of patience. Then and only then will you hear the words made popular by Sean Connery in the film "Finding Forrester" cheering you on, "You're the man now Dawg!"

CAN YOU WAIT FOR IT?

In concluding this lecture, I would state the following – even after you achieve patience, there will still be several miles of distance between you and your destiny. The question is – can you patiently wait for it?

I was speaking to a group of young women along these lines and asked them the following question – how many of you are looking for Mr. Right? Nearly everyone's hand shot up as they began clamoring about Mr. Right, figurative though he may be.

I then asked them a follow-up question inquiring, "How many of you are with someone right now?"

Again nearly everyone's hand shot up. However, I was not expecting this. So I looked at them all inquisitively and asked, "So you're with someone at this moment, but he's not Mr. Right – and you know this?"

Amazingly they all proceeded to nod, affirming what I had said was true.

By this time I was beside myself. So without a second thought I asked, "Then who is the man you're currently with?"

"Mr. Right-Now!" a young lady exclaimed as she and the entire class burst into laughter.

I laughed a bit too, but couldn't continue because I knew something about Mr. Right-Now. More often than not, he never transitions into Mr. Right because he is content with the temporary pleasures of short-term relationships. For that reason, he will not generally be inclined to commit to one woman; rather he will continually desire to be Mr. Right-Now for as many women as possible (and at the same time if he can pull this charade off).

I told them this and then some. See although I was a happily married man and had never operated in the model of Mr. Right-Now, I knew several men who did. So I let them in on some not-so-good intentions of Mr. Right-Now which obviously got their attention.

I then told them perhaps the most important thing about Mr. Right. With a faint hint of desperation I said to them, "He's looking for you the same way you are looking for him. The only question is – what are you going to do when Mr. Right finally shows up only to find you're with Mr. Right-Now?"

Again the room became deathly silent. If you haven't noticed by now, I have an uncanny way of turning a boisterous crowd into a group of silent sheep. All it takes is a pointed question that makes them think about what they're saying. Next comes the inflexion. Then comes the silence – peaceful minds are now in thought.

Now upon seeing no one was prepared to respond to my inquiry, I asked a final follow-up question to conclude my point and seal the deal. There I inquired, "After all the wonderful things you have said about Mr. Right and the perfect life you are destined to have with him, why would you so willingly risk this amazing future with him for a temporary fling with Mr. Right-Now?"

Again no one responded. It's usually at this point in the discussion that my group is prepared to listen to what I have to tell them completely and without any prejudice or preconceptions. So I proceeded to share with them more of my knowledge of Mr. Right-Now.

"The truth is there is nothing funny about Mr. Right-Now," I said. Then I continued, "The truth is he is one of many tragic characters in life who will only bring tragedy into yours if you let him. The only question is – will you let him? Or will you stay on your path to fulfillment and patiently wait for Mr. Right?"

This discourse reveals a crucial fact about Mr. Right-Now; that is he pulls women off of their path to fulfillment because he himself is unfulfilled. Accordingly, women are unwisely settling every time they choose to be with Mr. Right-Now – and although it is unknown to many, settling is one of the many slippery slopes associated with the quest for fulfillment, all of which are extremely dangerous; for once you begin settling for less in one area of your life, you will begin settling for less in others.

I don't know how many of those young women in the group actually took my advice to heart and made the necessary changes in their lives. But I do know this – based upon their reaction to my message, they were never going to look at Mr. Right-Now the same way again.

What about you? Even if your situation is altogether different from this example, you still can not afford to settle when it comes to your path to fulfillment. I believe I've provided ample evidence to this end thus far in the composition and I will provide even more in the next chapter.

Notwithstanding, what is crucial to understand at this juncture is this – settling will cause you to slide further and further away from your destiny faster than any other path associated with this life. So take my advice and avoid it at all costs.

Likewise don't be tired by your patient waiting; for even though it will often feel like you are waiting for your destiny, the truth is your destiny is almost always waiting on you. So do not fail to progress your quest for fulfillment, for you are enduring critical processes which are all working to fashion you for your destiny – and then your time will come.

THE SUMMATION

Patience is one of the most difficult levels of the Pinnacle of Purpose because there's no telling how long it will take for us to finally walk into our destiny. Therefore, we must always realize the truest purpose of patience is not to weary us with endless waiting; rather it is to empower us to endure every season structured to prepare us for this awesome experience.

Furthermore, patience remains the greatest investment you can make in yourself and others. Truly abiding your time in this wise is one of the greatest things you'll ever do. Accordingly, once you master this age-old principle, you will only be one step away from achieving purpose and living the life you've always imagined. Here's the final word on patience.

The key to patience is time management. Therefore, as long as you allocate your time appropriately, you will find yourself consistently occupied instead of restlessly waiting on your destiny to arrive – and then you will see it. The door to your *forever* is clear. All you have to do is take a deep breath and walk inside.

CHAPTER 12

Peace

*

*"It came to pass that as I prayed, I found that in
my heart was made; A peacefulness which could
not part, and left the cot where I had laid."*

INSULATED AGAINST DISTRESS

Before concluding this composition, I would offer one final lecture on the seventh and final level of purpose. That would be peace, the objective of which is to transform us into individuals who are able to remain calm, cool, and collected in the midst of unlimited circumstances. For this cause, my favorite example of peace is the eye of the storm, a small area of tranquility directly in the center of a tropical storm.

Elevating this model to our quest for fulfillment, the eye of the storm represents the phase in our quest where we are continually at peace regardless of the situations we find ourselves in. This is an amazing reality to be sure, for we live in a troubled world characterized by persistent storms and conflict.

This is precisely why peace is so critical, for the storms of life are ever-present. Nevertheless, this disconcerting fact is not the most important matter. On the contrary, the most important matter evolves from this simple question – knowing there will be storms in your life, how are you going to deal with them?

Now some people think they can outrun the storms in their lives. Believe me; I know. I've tried and learned a crucial lesson in the disastrous process; that is you can't outrun trouble no matter how hard you try. Even with my catlike reflexes, I found this to be impossible simply because trouble is everywhere.

Furthermore, even if we try to evade trouble or put off issues we don't want to deal with, the latter end will always be worse than if we had just tackled them head-on. Therefore, we must be determined to deal with every manner of conflict immediately and, at the same time, with great patience. We call it being fast but not in a hurry.

In doing so, we will make an amazing discovery; namely this – the key to handling conflict lies solely in our ability to ensure the conflict ends in peace. In effect, the peace we have within us is applied to every situation we find ourselves in. Definitively this is the only way we will be able to retain our peace while remaining insulated against distress.

PROTECTING YOUR PERSONAL SPACE

This realism lends itself to another facet of the eye of the storm called the eyewall, a crucial boundary which allows the eye to remain calm in the midst of violent winds.

Applying this example to our quest for fulfillment, our eyewall represents the boundary around our personal space. This is crucial because it is impossible for us to have peace apart from this boundary. On the rather, if we allow negativity in any form to compromise this space, we will gradually lose our peace while taking on avoidable conflict, pressures, and stress.

Upon understanding this reality, most of us will be forced to take drastic yet crucial actions in the order of removing all the negative energy from our personal space. Otherwise, in the course of time, the negative energy which we allowed to remain is going to compromise our peace and prevent us from fulfilling our purpose.

Observably the greatest source of negative energy we endure comes from people. Yet contrary to the obvious, these people aren't necessarily our enemies or strangers. Ironically the greatest measures of negative energy we experience come from our so-called friends and members of our extended family.

Reason being, we don't typically allow our enemies or strangers into our personal space because we readily perceive their potential threat to our well-being. Thus we naturally (often subconsciously) take actions to insulate ourselves against them. We call it being guarded.

Notwithstanding, we do not usually take this approach with our friends and family – and because we often put more trust in them than they are worthy of, they are oddly enough the greatest sources of distress in our lives.

For that reason, some of these people must be eliminated from your personal space if you are determined to live a life of purpose and find fulfillment; particularly those who are constantly bringing negative energies into your life.

MAKING THE CUT

I surmise we'll have little trouble cutting off 1/3 of these individuals because we already perceive how these informal relationships are typically phony or non-literal. Besides this, we usually become wiser the older we get and will eventually come to know who's really "got our back." So here's the question of the hour — who are the remaining 2/3 of those we will need to exclude from our personal space?

I'll begin answering this question by first tackling another 1/3 of your personal "cut list." That would be extended members of your family.

First of all, let me state that I am not an advocate of breaking up families or causing division between loved ones. However, I am an advocate of progressive living and have learned from personal experience that members of a dysfunctional family are often the greatest threats to your peace. Consequently, they are often some of the final blockers on your path to fulfillment. So here's another question for this hour — are you going to clear them or are you going to let them stand in your way?

In my own life I chose the latter. See certain members of my extended family were not only taking away my peace; they were having a negative impact on the functional family I was trying to raise. Accordingly, there was more at stake than just my peace. The future of my family was also in play.

Now you might find it difficult to understand the gravity of this example if you've never been in this situation. Nevertheless, I am quite sure you could perceive the difficulty in the decision I had to make and why it took me years to make it, for I persistently hoped things would get better.

Then one day it finally hit me — things weren't getting better. They were only getting worse and would continue to get worse as long as varying family members were committed to carrying on the dysfunctional behaviors which have divided and persistently ruined our extended family.

This realism is a testament to the disastrous yet certain end of any relationship in which at least one of the individuals is persistently regressive. Inevitably these relationships will never advance. They will only get worse until the progressive individual reaches their breaking point and is unable to remain in the relationship as it stands.

Regrettably this is what befell me in my life. After years of being negatively impacted by dysfunctional family members, one incident finally pushed me over the edge – and although I didn't understand it immediately, I eventually realized why this single instance effectually broke the bow. Here's why – I had finally reached the level of peace and was preparing to walk the final mile in my personal quest for fulfillment.

Logistically speaking, I arrived at a fork in the road where I could either continue on the path which led to my destiny or continue my attempt to maintain broken family relationships. It was there at that crossing that I came to the following conclusion – in order to walk the final steps on this path, I was going to have to put distance between myself and certain family members in order to protect my personal space from their persistent negativity.

WHEN THINGS ARE NOT THE SAME

Now what I find remarkable at this time is that I (like many true family advocates) was able and willing to endure negative energies from certain family members for the better part of my quest for fulfillment for a truly heroic cause – I believed (more likely hoped) that somehow I could get through to them with my positive energy and the pure soundness of my consistent message of progressive relations. For whatever reason, this never happened.

Nevertheless, I am glad I fought this fight as long as I was physically, spiritually, and emotionally able to. It made the difficult decision to put distance between myself and certain family members easier.

It was also helpful that I was able to talk about what I was going through with someone who had been through a similar situation. While having lunch with a colleague, we began discussing the current chapters in our lives. I was in the early stages of initiating Life Pinnacles while she was starting a new management position for an IT firm in the city.

I'm not sure how we got on the topic, but I found myself laying it all out to her; specifically the episode I had recently endured and how I had finally brought myself to take a demonstrative stand for myself and my peace.

As I relayed everything to her, I remember her closing her eyes as she shook her head. I didn't realize it then, but at that moment her mind went back to a time when she had endured a similar season in her life with her family.

After I finally stopped talking, she looked at me closely and said, "Del, I've been there." She then exhaled and repeated herself saying, "I've been there."

"Really? So what did you do?" I asked inquisitively because I almost always (if not always) get great advice from my female colleagues. Then again I, like so many others, had never considered how I was truly not alone (an oversight we often make when we are going through difficult times).

She looked at me closely and replied, "I did what I had to do and the same thing you did. I put distance between us because although they didn't realize it, they were ruining my life."

She then went on to give me a high-level account of the tragedy which befell her. I could see the emotional discomfort on her face as she talked about it. It was almost as if she was reliving that troublesome time.

However, it was clear to me that she was not overly distressed by the situation or her unavoidable decision to distance herself from certain family members. On the contrary, she was yet disappointed with her family's true colors as well as the way things turned out because of them.

I then asked her, "What's the point of all this? Are they maliciously trying to ruin my life or is it something they're doing subconsciously?"

"It's about control Del," she said. "It's all about control."

She then pointed out to me several aspects of the story I had shared with her in which control was obviously in play (foul play that is). These were aspects which I had not considered because I was going through this for the first time. Yet she could point them out effortlessly because she had already overcome what I was suffering.

Upon settling her discourse about control she concluded, "After your family accepts the fact that you are your own person with your own destiny and that they can't control you, they'll chill out. Until then, you have to stay focused on accomplishing everything you were designed to do in your life. If your family or friends can't accept and support you in the process, then they're not leaving you with too much of a choice. But there is still a choice to be made and you have to make it yourself; because if you don't, then no one will."

I nodded as I considered every word she said. That's when she began shaking her head again. I perceived her mind was going back to her experience with her family, so I asked her if she didn't mind sharing her thoughts.

"I know what you're going through," she told me with a faint shade of pain in her voice, "it's hard, Del. It's real hard. It's nothing you'd wish on your worst enemy."

She began shaking her head again, so I joined her; lamenting the fact that 2 young professionals, successful in their own right, would endure such shallow and shady verses from their families. That's when I asked her how she got through it.

"Prayer," she said as a smile finally came to her face, "lots of prayer... and my husband. He was my rock. He showered me with positive reinforcement and reminded me constantly that I was not to blame for what happened... But I tried so hard to make it work. Del, I tried so hard..."

I'll never forget the look on her face when said, *"I tried so hard."* Neither will I forget how a chill went down my back when she did, for at that moment she looked exactly how I felt – hopeless, the empty feeling one gets after they've exhausted all of their energies and resources; yet to no avail. The whole thing still falls apart. We fought with fate and on this occasion fate won.

Now as she went on to tell me how she overcame this inescapable fallout in her life, one question kept looming in the back of my mind. So once she concluded, I took a deep breath and asked her my final question on that day. With an unshakable measure of apprehension I inquired, "So how does it end?"

"Oh they come back," she told me, then continuing, "After they realize that they can't break you, they learn to accept you."

"Really?" I asked shocked, for at that point in time I couldn't even fathom a future scenario in which they would even attempt to reconnect on any terms; specifically because of the damage which had been done.

"Yes," she said nodding, "they do come back. However, it's not the same and it will never be the same because certain lines have been crossed. You'll forgive them, sure, because that's who you are. But it's almost impossible to recapture the levels of trust and kinship you had prior to the fallout; especially if they really haven't changed, and most of the times they haven't. They've just given up on harassing you because they've realized it's not going to work. You have peace with who you are and what you are doing. They will fight you no longer, true; but your relationship, Del, with your family… it will never be the same."

Although I was somewhat unprepared to consider this reality, the truth is that deep down inside I already knew it to be true. There are various acts and occasions that will have permanent impacts on progressive relationships; specifically when and if the relationship should survive. Since families are bonded by blood, the relationship (as dysfunctional as it may be) will always be there. It just won't be the same.

YOUR BREAKING POINT

I would at this time state my opinion – if you're in a situation in which members of your family or your so-called friends are persistently bringing negative energies into your personal space, you should do your best to coexist with them. It's a valiant show really; you providing them with a heroic display of patience and peace while showing them the value of honesty, trust, communication, and all the other facets of progressive relations.

However, you must also realize that you will eventually reach your breaking point if the persons in question do not change their dysfunctional behaviors – and that's the time you must make your move. Ready or not, that's the time you'll need to make another cut.

Like me, you may find yourself making these cuts at the level of peace. In other cases, you may find yourself making substantial cuts from the beginning of your quest until the very end. Either or, you should not invest excess time and energy attempting to maintain broken relationships, for it is impossible to have a progressive relationship with someone who is clearly not progressing.

This matter lends itself to a crucial realism associated with your destiny; that is your path to fulfillment will always deviate from the paths which dysfunctional family members and other regressive individuals are traveling.

This is precisely why many of them will end up hating on you. Due to their dysfunctional and regressive behavior, they are often to some degree miserable – and what do we know about misery? Does not misery love company? Yet seeing as you are not miserable (rather you are being fulfilled), what company do you have with those who are both miserable and insistent upon their ways?

Unfortunately this is one of the primary reasons why they are so adverse to you fulfilling your destiny. It's because your fulfillment is an indictment against their depressed reality, a reality which they've acquired by their failure to invest in the progressive path you are treading.

For this cause, they will unwarrantedly (and often without any pre-calculation) spend a good majority of their efforts tearing you down as opposed to lifting you up. Don't be discouraged by this; neither be taken aback, for if they had the personal resolve to lift anyone up they would lift themselves up. Yet they can not.

For that reason, they do not deserve your indignation or any retaliation for any of their suspect actions. If anything they deserve your prayers and whatever support you are able to provide without compromising your peace. After all, we are talking about family here. They may take the low road, but you should always hope for the best and do everything within your power to see hope through. In the end this may be all you're able to do.

I would state my beliefs in concluding this matter. If this depiction describes your family in any way, shape, or form, it's safe to say they don't make the cut. You must keep them from your personal space if you are to fulfill your purpose. I wish you all the best.

CLEARING THE NOISE

Moving on, even if you are forced to cut certain family members out of your personal space, this cut (along with your preliminary cut of the nonproductive relationships in your life) only accounts for approximately 2/3 of the relationships you must discard to have peace. As for the remaining 1/3, they do not actually fit any particular mold. Still they all have one thing in common – they increase the noise in your life.

What is noise in this context? Definitively noise represents all the things you hear and consider which do not help you progress your quest for fulfillment. Rather these non-value added matters will always slow you down and often cause you to become distracted.

> *The majority of the people in our lives are either unable to understand or unwilling to accept our destiny. Therefore, as they cannot effectively help us achieve our destiny, they will often unintentionally work to pull us away from it.*

Along these lines, the obvious detriment of noise lies in the fact that it increases the difficulty in staying focused. Accordingly, the more noise we have in our lives, the more susceptible we are to losing sight of our purpose and ultimately deviating from our path to fulfillment. This brings us to our next interest point.

This matter shouldn't be too difficult to understand. How many of you have parents who picked your profession for you before you had an opportunity to voice the profession of your desire? Or how many of you have had friends who were always seemingly trying to get you to do things you didn't really want to do? I had both and let me tell you, it wasn't easy.

Then I made an amazing discovery — neither my friends nor my family were purposefully trying to keep me from my destiny. They were just trying to control me; namely to achieve objectives which were either aligned with their personal desires for me or things they wanted from me.

All in all, many of these matters did not correspond with my purpose. Else there would never have been a power struggle for control over the evolution of *my life*. Every interaction would have been natural and within the flow of my destiny; thus eliminating the conflict.

Yet seeing as there was ample conflict, I have come to the following conclusion — anyone who tries to control me in any manner is only doing so because they do not accept who I am. Therefore, they will consistently work to change me via control until I unhappily become the person they want me to be for their selfish reasons.

This speaks to a critical aspect of friendship. Like all relationships, the goal of friendship is not to use your friends to achieve your desires. Contrariwise, the goal of friendship is to support your friend as he or she walks their individual path to fulfillment.

Sure there are times when you will need to help your friends out of a sticky situation or go out of your way to pick them up, but this should not be the definition of your friendship. On the contrary, your friendship should be defined by predominately progressive experiences for both parties. The occasions where you have to carry your friends should be the exceptions to the rule, not the norm. Less you find yourself surrounded by excess noise and persistently distracted even after making the vast majority of your cuts.

Therefore, seeing as this is a crucial matter, I will leave you with these final words on this discussion; crucial words of wisdom which I say to my children every night before they go to bed – now, no more noise.

THE POWER OF POSITIVE INFLUENCE

Now the primary reason why we are cutting various people out of our personal space is not for the sake of downsizing our life. It's because the only way to find peace is to regularly tap into the unlimited power of positive influence, and the best way to do this is by incorporating positive people into your life. These are going to replace those you were forced to cut out.

This is crucial because the positive energy emitting from within your newfound friends will connect with and amplify the positive energy within you. This will effectually provide you with even greater measures of positive energy to inject within each of your life offices.

I can attest to this reality because I see it every day in my life and in the lives of others who have learned this lesson. For me it starts at home, then follows me to work, and everywhere I go; it doesn't matter. I have armed myself with awesome levels of positive energy and I routinely see the terrific effects it has on those around me, effects too many to tell.

Here's the thing though – this positive energy has to be legit, evolving from an authentic source of peace. Trust me; most people can recognize a fraud a mile away and they will call you out on it. Nevertheless, if you truly have peace, your positive energy will be real. Everyone around you will feel it and many will regularly tap into it.

Eventually they will become somewhat dependent on you; specifically your consistent and increasingly positive nature. See you're like a lifeline, an everyday helping hand to all who know you, and a random act of kindness just waiting to happen.

Subsequently, when someone needs a friend or just someone to lift them up, they're going to look for you first; not because your advice is going to be infinitely better than anyone else's. Rather they're going to look for you because your advice is going to be wrapped in terrific measures of positive energy, enough to bring crucial, much needed strands of peace and reassurance into their life.

This speaks to a crucial matter concerning constructive criticism; namely there is a way to deliver criticism such that it is indeed constructive. Have you ever had someone yell criticisms at you because they were upset at you for a matter? I have and can testify that this manner of delivery is hardly constructive.

Moreover, even if the criticism is legitimate, the delivery will often ruin the intended message and prevent the criticism from being constructive. This is precisely why it is so important to always be positive, even when you are forced to censure someone for their betterment. Else you will be labeled as out-of-control or a hothead, and no one will desire to be around you; let alone come to you for advice.

Needless to say, providing sound advice in a positive manner is a model way of life; for it not only provides edification for those in need, it also provides edification for you as a reliable source of comfort and strength for many within your life offices.

Visibly it's a cycle, a persistent release and flow of positive energy between multiple parties which both begins and ends with peace. This flow is what I strive for in my life. It is what every purpose seeker dreams of for each of their offices, and many of us either live here or are well on our way.

Going further, positive influences effectively push us towards our destiny. This matter lends itself to our eyewall (i.e. the barrier around our personal space). Explicitly, the source of our eyewall is positive energy. Thus masterfully, in every adverse occasion the various positive influences in our lives will safeguard us from distress and keep us moving forward towards our destiny.

Manifestly the power of negative influences lies in the inverse; for instead of pushing us towards our destiny, these contrary factors work to either pull us back or push us further away. This is why you'll almost always find yourself cutting more people out of your personal space than inviting them into it. Sadly, because of excess negative influences, there are more people in our world who have the greater potential of preventing you from rising to your destiny than assisting you in your fulfillment.

Here is the conclusion of this matter – the most important person in your life is you. So ask yourself this question – if I don't protect myself from the devastating effects of negative influences, then who will?

THE SELF-FULFILLING PROPHECY

Moving on, you should do more than just surround yourself with true friends who continually inundate your personal space with positive energy. You yourself have to be the most positive person in your life as this is the only way you will be able to cash in on *"The Self-fulfilling Prophecy,"* a crucial life lesson which reveals the following:

If you repeat anything long enough and often enough on your path to fulfillment, it will transpire.

This is yet more evidence that we are going to find it nearly impossible to have peace apart from positive reinforcement. Thus we should all get into the habit of regularly making confident declarations about our destiny and complementing ourselves within reason.

Now the key here is *within reason*. See I'm not for making positive declarations just for the sake of being positive, for positivity alone does not foster peace. Decisively, positivity must be centered on truth; particularly those truths which you have discovered about yourself from the beginning interval of your quest until now.

In my case, I woke up every morning not only telling myself I would fulfill my destiny. I also told myself why; explicitly because I was dedicated to mastering and employing confidence, knowledge, good judgment, sound work ethic, focus, patience, and peace.

Now I spelled it out to this degree simply because I needed to regularly remind myself of what it would take to achieve my goal. So when things got hard, I didn't just tell myself it would get better. I knew exactly why.

Here's the clincher – this process worked perfectly because I had already determined my life purposes. So my positive reaffirmation was in line with initiatives I was well able to accomplish and, advantageously, I was able to see the results of my efforts on a regular basis.

All the same, this would not have worked if either my efforts or my declarations were unaligned with my destiny. See I wasn't declaring that I'd be a world-class swimmer or the first astronaut from my neighborhood; neither did I waste one minute of my time towards these initiatives. No sir; all my energies were directed towards one thing and one thing alone – fulfilling my purpose and ultimately my destiny at all costs.

To be quite candid, this is the primary reason why I'm where I'm at today. It's because I never gave up no matter how demanding the path became. How could I? I'd already concluded that there is no easy path in life, not one of all the thousands.

However, of all these paths, I was convinced there was at least one which offers enduring fulfillment and success. Subsequently, why wouldn't I invest all my energies and resources towards understanding and walking this path until I reached the end and obtained my prize?

Perhaps you applaud my dedication but can not bring yourself to this level of commitment without concrete evidence outlining how you will obtain your prize in detailed fashion. You see that's the thing. So many like you are unconvinced a life of purpose and fulfillment can be theirs simply because they don't see how it could happen.

This is precisely why the model of the Pinnacle of Purpose is so effective, for it decisively reveals how each purpose seeker can find the fulfillment they are looking for. All you have to do is follow the path from confidence to peace and you will arrive at the destination you seek.

As for the details (i.e. the coveted possession of all those lacking faith), you're not going to have access to them prior to any life episode. Thus it is not some unique attribute of the path to fulfillment. It's a universal characteristic of life, for there is no path in life which provides this manner of detailed foreshadowing. It's a myth if there ever was one.

Therefore, do not allow yourself to become mired in the details. All this will do is increase your levels of doubt and eventually cause you to come to the conclusion that you are unable to fulfill your purpose – and you won't; yet another testament to the self-fulfilling prophecy.

LETTING IT GO

In concluding this chapter and this composition, I would like to speak to the final mile associated with our mastery of peace; a critical juncture where we let it all go. That is to say, we let go of any negative feelings, emotions, or motivations we may have retained until this closing interval; specifically negative energies from within.

Now there are numerous ways these energies develop internally. However, the most prominent manner occurs during the process in which we turn the throwing stones of our detractors into our stepping stones. In each occurrence we would have fatefully held onto to the stepping stone.

This is problematic because the stepping stone was originally a throwing stone. Thus it has a negative source and will prevent us from rising to our destiny if we are yet holding on to it, for all things negative are as dead weight and have no potential of lifting us up towards our destiny.

What they do have is the deadly potential to hold us back by subjecting us to additional unnecessary pressures and stress. This is precisely why we can't dwell on any of the negative occasions of our past after we have effectively converted each into a positive experience which helped us get to where we are going.

I experienced this wake-up call not long ago. See I was convinced I had mastered every level of the Pinnacle of Purpose, from confidence all the way to peace. Yet I was still waiting for an opportunity to present itself for me to fulfill my destiny. I remember asking myself on a daily basis, "What am I lacking?"

Then one day I began to thoroughly consider all the things I had overcome to get to where I was at. It was exactly then that I realized I wasn't lacking anything. However, I was unknowingly holding onto negative energy which had evolved internally due to my persistent dwelling on those things I had overcome and people I had proven wrong.

Allow me to explain. Over time I encountered a handful of people who decided it was in their best interest to throw stones at me; no shock there.

So I converted each throwing stone into a stepping stone as I have described earlier in this composition.

Yet even though I was successful in this endeavor, I incurred a self-inflicting wound simply because I allowed the disdain behind each stone thrown to be a driving factor in my quest. In essence, I wasn't just trying to be successful for me. I was also motivated to prove my disparagers wrong.

> **The longer you continue to allow negative impulses to drive you towards progressive goals, the greater that negative influence becomes.**

Here's the thing – the "prove-them-wrong" approach might *work* for a while, but it never works long-term. The reason behind this truism is another interest point.

Accordingly, if we allow ourselves to be driven by negative forces, we will find it impossible to obtain peace in full; for as we dwell on these negative energies, we are giving these adverse forces greater power. This leaves us with less power to exert towards the positive energies required to carry us towards progressive goals; explicitly our destiny.

For this cause, we must always forgive those who have thrown stones at us; ideally when the stone is first thrown and even if they never apologize for it. Remember – you're on the path to fulfillment. That makes you the bigger person. So be who you are. Be the bigger person and forgive.

Likewise we must not dwell on the past; primarily any occasion which is negative in its origin. Markedly it's one of the few occasions in life where you really need to have a short-term memory, for even the recent past is yet in the past.

Does that mean you will forget? Maybe not. However, you can choose not to think on negative things if you are willing to discipline your mind. After which, you will find yourself being driven by purely positive impulses.

Definitively this will be validated by the fact that you're not trying to prove anyone wrong – and why should you? Haters don't throw stones at us because of our issues. They throw stones at us because of their issues.

As I said before, haters are some of the most tragic losers in life. So let me ask you a pointed question – what in the world are you trying to prove to them? What do they even know about you? Obviously they don't know much or they wouldn't be so adverse to you fulfilling your purpose.

Thankfully I realized this and found it to be the final major action I needed to take before finally crossing over into my destiny and living a life of purpose. There I was, standing on top of my personal pinnacle of purpose, the metaphoric apex of the leading mountain in a series of highlands and peaks which constitute my destiny – and as I surveyed this wondrous sight, I closed my eyes, took a deep breath, and I let it all go.

I then looked around and said to myself, "I'm here… I'm finally here."

It was exactly then that every trace of negative energy I had unknowingly held onto immediately vanished, for I had bravely overcome everything which stood in between me and my destiny and was only a few moments from living the life I've always imagined. In a personal space within this great big world dedicated to my purpose, carved out exclusively for me, I will not only be dreaming my dreams. I will begin living my dreams, and experiencing life in ways I've never imagined.

There I made a promise to myself declaring, "From this day forward, I will no longer live to prove anyone wrong, for now I can see that everyone who speaks against my destiny is already wrong. So there's nothing for me to prove.

I will only be filled with positive energies and will labor each day to bring light into every environment I am blessed to see; for I am letting it all go now – and now, I am finally at peace."

THE SUMMATION

As the closing level of the Pinnacle of Purpose, peace is the final lesson we must learn before we finally solve our personal mystery, become one with our destiny, and effectively begin living an authentic life of purpose.

This is one of many reasons why so many desire peace. Although some do not realize it, peace is the prevailing validation of our undivided fulfillment and continued success. Hence peace is where it's at. Peace is where you want to be.

Nevertheless, you are going to have to eliminate certain people from your personal space to get there; specifically those who persistently bring you down via their negative energy.

Some of these may be family members. Some of these may be friends. In every case you must do what's best for you for the following cause – if you don't, then no one will. This brings me to my final word on peace.

Of all the things you must do to have peace, never forget to engulf yourself daily with positive reinforcement and declarations of your impending future. These will not only insulate you against every opposition and turn of fate; decisively, they will carry you all the way to the top of your personal pinnacle of purpose and into the awesome realm of your destiny.

CONCLUSION

*

In concluding this series of lectures on some of the most imperative topics regarding the existence of man, I applaud all those who have invested the time to not only consider the points of view offered in this composition; but who have also come to understand the immense value associated with the omnipresent call to living a life of purpose.

From where I stand, if you truly appreciate the significance of this worthy cause, you have already packed your bags and are preparing to set off on your personal quest for fulfillment. Therefore, I would like to provide you with a few more words of advice to ensure you have the most profitable journey.

First of all, this compilation is a guide which focuses on the high-level path and principles associated with living a life of purpose. It does not dive into the details. Subsequently, you will come to various questions, challenges, and the like which are not perfectly addressed in this work at the detailed level (even so they are resolved by the principles I have lectured on).

In these occasions, I advise each purpose seeker to get in contact with a qualified party to work out any situation which must be addressed at a finer level and requires dedicated counseling. That includes Life Pinnacles, for counseling and life coaching are 2 services which we provide.

Secondly, I would remind each purpose seeker that you are not going to find fulfillment overnight. It's a process which, depending on how far you've migrated away from your truest life purposes, may take years to complete.

Do not be discouraged by this reality. Rather be fortified by it. Be reinvigorated by it, for there is terrific value in the totality of the journey. Truly every step on this path bears its own measure of fulfillment and thus injects strands of self-actualization into each sojourner as they travel along their way.

Lastly, I want to encourage each seeker to rise to their moment and, upon rising, impressively take it all in; specifically once you ascend to the height of your purpose and, beholding the doors to your destiny, you enter in.

Then the lights come on. The stage is set. All the world is watching, waiting for you to do what you were designed to do. All the world is looking on intently to see if your example of purpose, fulfillment, and destiny is indeed true.

So what do you do? With a sense of terrific achievement, you take a deep breath and wholly embrace the eternal magnitude of your moment – and then you show them something special. You show them something magnificent, something so extraordinary that they will never forget it as long as they live.

My dear friends, conclusively and with great authority, you show them what it looks like when you solve the world's greatest mystery – you.

APPENDIX A

*

"Opportunity," by Edward Rowland Sill (1841-1887)

This I beheld, or dreamed it in a dream:--
There spread a cloud of dust along a plain;
And underneath the cloud, or in it, raged
A furious battle, and men yelled, and swords
Shocked upon swords and shields. A prince's banner
Wavered, then staggered backward, hemmed by foes.
A craven hung along the battle's edge,
And thought, "Had I a sword of keener steel--
That blue blade that the king's son bears, -- but this
Blunt thing--!" he snapped and flung it from his hand,
And lowering crept away and left the field.
Then came the king's son, wounded, sore bestead,
And weaponless, and saw the broken sword,
Hilt-buried in the dry and trodden sand,
And ran and snatched it, and with battle shout
Lifted afresh he hewed his enemy down,
And saved a great cause that heroic day.

ABOUT THE AUTHOR

*

D. L. Anderson is an author and speaker whose passion is to teach varying life principles which have the ability to make profound impacts on the lives of others. For information about D. L. Anderson's books or professional speaking services, to sign up for his mailings, or to share how this book has affected your life, please email D. L. Anderson at <u>dlanderson@ lifepinnacles.com</u>.

COMING IN 2015

*

"Unlocking the Mystery of You, The Pinnacle of Purpose," is the first book in this series which I, the author, am referring to as, *"The Pinnacles of Life"* book series. The next book in this series will be entitled, ***"Unleashing Your Maximum Potential, The Pinnacle of Excellence."***

In this book we will take the next step forward in our over-arching quest for fulfillment and discuss the vast importance of excellence in this pivotal procedure. Visit my website at www.lifepinnacles.com to learn more and to pre-order your copy.